THE ENCYCLOPEDIA of BIBLE CRAFTS for Preschoolers

Group

Loveland, Colorado

Group's R.E.A.L. Guarantee® to you:

This Group resource incorporates our R.E.A.L. approach to ministry—one that encourages long-term retention and life transformation. It's ministry that's:

Relational
Because learner-to-learner interaction enhances learning and builds Christian friendships.

Experiential
Because what learners experience through discussion and action sticks with them up to 9 times longer than what they simply hear or read.

Applicable
Because the aim of Christian education is to equip learners to be both hearers and doers of God's Word.

Learner-based
Because learners understand and retain more when the learning process takes into consideration how they learn best.

The Encyclopedia of BIBLE CRAFTS for Preschoolers

Copyright © 2004 by Group Publishing, Inc.

Visit our Web site: **www.group.com**

Credits
Contributing Authors: Linda A. Anderson, Ruthie Daniels, Heather A. Eades, Enelle G. Eder, Cindy S. Hansen, Jan Kershner, Carol Mader, Barbie Murphy, Elaine Ernst Schneider, Larry Shallenberger, and JanMarie Thompson
Editor: Jody Brolsma
Chief Creative Officer: Joani Schultz
Copy Editor: Lyndsay E. Gerwing
Art Director: Kari K. Monson
Illustrator: Jan Knudson
Print Production Artists: Pat Miller and Tracy K. Hindman
Cover Art Director: Jean Bruns
Cover Photographer: Daniel Treat
Production Manager: Peggy Naylor

Unless otherwise noted, Scripture taken from the HOLY BIBLE, NEW INTERNATIONAL VERSION®. Copyright © 1973, 1978, 1984 International Bible Society. Used by permission of Zondervan Publishing House. All rights reserved.

Library of Congress Cataloging-in-Publication Data
The encyclopedia of Bible crafts for preschoolers.
    p. cm.
    Includes indexes.
    ISBN 0-7644-2621-4
    1. Bible crafts. 2. Christian education of preschool children. 3. Bible–Study and teaching (Preschool)–-Activity programs.
    I. Group Publishing.
BS613.E535 2004
268'.432--dc21

          2003011362

10 9 8 7   13 12 11 10 09 08 07
Printed in the United States of America.

CONTENTS

INTRODUCTION

In the beginning of class, Jane created her world. Oh, it didn't turn out looking like the magnificent perfect world that God originally created. But it was Jane's world just the same, cut from various colors of craft foam and glued together seemingly at random onto a misshapen circle. Jane, a preschooler, was the beaming creator as she ran to show her mom at the end of class. "Look, Mommy! God made the world, and so did I! Will you hang it from my ceiling when we get home?"

Many preschoolers are just like Jane. They're excited to explore God's Word through all their senses—creating, smelling, baking, squishing, and tasting! *The Encyclopedia of Bible Crafts for Preschoolers* provides you with nearly 200 proven crafts from major Bible stories in the Old and New Testaments. You'll find "WOWS That Work" tips to help you extend learning and creating, an index that will help enhance your Bible lessons when using FaithWeaver™ Bible Curriculum or Hands-On Bible Curriculum™, easy step-by-step instructions for leaders, and a "Preschool Connection" section that will help make Bible learning a REAL experience.

The Encyclopedia of Bible Crafts for Preschoolers is an essential tool for any preschool teacher interested in helping children explore and understand the Bible. You can use this book with your Sunday school, children's church, midweek meetings, home schooling, Christian preschool programs, or any other time preschoolers are gathered together. So get ready for unique, motivating crafts that will inspire your children to learn about the Bible in no time!

The "Easy Steps" boxes are photocopiable so that your preschool helpers can follow them to help children create amazing crafts. We suggest that you enlarge the copies about 300 percent for easier readability.

GENESIS

GOD MADE THE WORLD
Genesis 1:1–31

What Kids Will Do: Create three-dimensional panoramic scenes of the creation of day and night, land and water.

What Kids Will Need: white poster board, colored construction paper, glue, crayons or markers, scissors (You may want to provide star stickers also.)

Preparation Place: Cut poster board into two 8x10-inch pieces. Make slits in the center of the *bottom* of one and the center of the *top* of the other. Hold the pages perpendicular to each other, and connect the two pieces by sliding the slits into each other.

EASY Steps CREATION CRAFTS

1. Give each child a poster board "book" that you made before class. Show children how to lay the book flat so two pages are facing them. Write, "God made daytime" across the two pages. Then instruct children to create a picture of daytime across the two pages by tearing construction paper into shapes such as sun, clouds, and blue sky. Let children glue the shapes to the pages.

2. Children may flip to another opening, where you'll write, "God made nighttime." Have children glue torn pieces of black construction paper to represent night. You may want to provide star stickers to add to the picture of night.

3. Let children open to two more pages. Write, "God made the land and plants." Children may tear construction paper to make trees, flowers, plants, and land. Help children glue the shapes to the poster board.

4. Let children open to the last two pages. Write, "God made the ocean." Have children tear blue construction paper to make the ocean and then tear paper to represent creatures that live in the sea. Children may glue these into the last blank pages.

PRESCHOOL CONNECTION

When children have finished, collect craft supplies. Read Genesis 1:1-23 aloud from the Bible so children know the passage is in God's Word. Then ask:

- **What is your favorite thing that God made?**

- **How can you thank God for making that?**

Say: **God has made so many wonderful things. You can use your panoramas to thank God for everything he made. Let's pray and thank God for such a wonderful world.**

As children pray, let them point to things they've added to their crafts and thank God for making those things.

GOD MADE THE WORLD

Genesis 1:1–31

What Kids Will Do: Use vegetables to make picture reminders of the vegetation God made.

What Kids Will Need: construction paper; paper towels; washable paint; shallow paper plates; forks; knife; vegetables and fruits such as broccoli, potatoes, green peppers, apples, oranges, and kiwi fruit

Preparation Place: Place a few folded paper towels on a paper plate. Pour a few tablespoons of paint onto the folded paper towels, and spread it around to saturate the "pad." Cut each fruit or vegetable so that a creative pattern is revealed. Stick a fork into the uncut side of the fruit or vegetable to create a handle for children to use.

 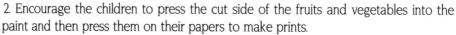

PLANT PRINTS

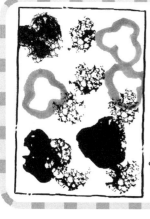

1. Show children the fruits and vegetables you've cut. Point out the interesting shapes and the seeds that are exposed in some of the fruit.

2. Encourage the children to press the cut side of the fruits and vegetables into the paint and then press them on their papers to make prints.

3. As children work, remind them that God made everything—even the plants that grow these fruits and vegetables!

PRESCHOOL CONNECTION

When children have finished their projects, collect craft supplies, and set the pictures aside to dry. Open your Bible to Genesis 1:11-13, and show children the words. Explain the story in your own preschool-friendly words. Ask:

- **Why do you think God made plants like the ones we used in our craft?**
- **How are these plants the same? How are they different?**
- **What is a favorite fruit or vegetable you like to eat?**

Say: **I'm so glad God made yummy fruits and vegetables! They taste good and help keep our bodies strong and healthy. When you look at your Plant Print, you might get hungry. Then you can eat some tasty fruits or vegetables and thank God for his wonderful creation!**

Bring in fruits and vegetables that you've washed and cut into bite-size pieces. Let children taste some of the fruit and vegetable pieces and thank God for this good food.

8

GOD MADE THE WORLD

Genesis 1:1–31

What Kids Will Do: Make three-dimensional animals or birds to remember the creatures God created.

What Kids Will Need: poster board, stapler, hole punch, chenille wires, tissue paper, construction paper, glue, colored markers, scissors, CD player, CD of fun children's music

Preparation Place: Cut poster board into 6x7-inch sheets. Roll each sheet into a tube and staple it. Use the hole punch to make two holes, opposite each other, at each end of the tube. Each child will need one tube.

EASY Steps — CRAFTY CREATURES

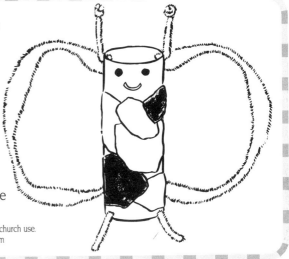

1. Give each child a cardboard tube, and write his or her name on it.

2. Encourage children to use tissue paper, chenille wires, or construction paper to create a bird or animal that God made. The possibilities are endless, so encourage each child to make something different from what anyone else is making.

3. Let children use markers to add features such as eyes, noses, mouths, or even scales.

4. Adam named the animals and birds, so encourage the children to name their creatures, too.

PRESCHOOL CONNECTION

When children have finished, collect craft supplies. Read Genesis 1:20-25 aloud from an easy-to-understand Bible translation so children know the passage is in God's Word. Then ask:

- **What kinds of animals did you make?**
- **How are your animals different from the ones God made?**
- **How can we thank God for all the wonderful animals and birds he made?**

Say: **God made a whole world filled with animals that crawl, fly, hop, swim, run, gallop, and slither! Each animal is different—just like all of your animals are different and special.**

Play some fun music and have a parade, carrying the craft creatures around your room.

GOD MADE PEOPLE
Genesis 1:26–31; 2:4–25

What Kids Will Do: Make pictures of themselves and decorate frames for them.

What Kids Will Need: 8½x11-inch pieces of light-colored construction paper, poster board, markers or crayons, glue, hole punch, yarn, scissors

Preparation Place: Make a poster board frame for each child, cut with an 8x10-inch opening. Punch two holes at the top of each frame for yarn to go through so children can hang the pictures. Set all other supplies on a table, within easy reach of the children.

EASY Steps

I AM MADE BY GOD

1. Give each child an 8½x11-inch piece of light-colored construction paper. Write the child's name on the back of the paper.

2. Talk briefly about how God made us with arms, legs, bodies, heads, and faces. Then encourage children to draw pictures of themselves.

3. After children have finished their drawings, give them each a frame to decorate. Help children glue the frames over their self-portraits. Write, "God Made Me" on each frame.

4. Direct children to thread yarn through the punched holes to make a hanger.

WOWS that work

Lead children in this song, sung to the tune of "Head and Shoulders." Encourage children to touch each body part as it is mentioned in the song.

Head and shoulders, knees
  and toes, knees and toes,
  knees and toes,
And eyes, and ears, and
  mouth, and nose;
God made us special, don't
  you know?

PRESCHOOL CONNECTION

When children have finished, collect craft supplies. Open your Bible to Genesis 1:26-27 so children know the passage is in God's Word. Then explain the story in your own preschool-friendly words. Then ask:

· **Why do you think God made you?**

· **What is special about how God made you?**

· **What is something special about how God made the person sitting next to you?**

Say: **The Bible tells us that God made people and made each one special. God made your eyes, your nose, and your toes! God loves each part of you. You are so special to God!**

Encourage the children to hang their pictures on the walls in their bedrooms to remind them that God made each of them special.

GOD MADE PEOPLE
Genesis 1:26–31; 2:4–25

What Kids Will Do: Use craft sticks to make pictures of their families.

What Kids Will Need: large craft sticks, fine-tipped markers, 8½x11-inch sheets of poster board or cardboard, glue

Preparation Place: Make a sample craft of you and your family. Then set out all of the supplies where children can easily reach them.

EASY Steps   GOD MADE MY FAMILY

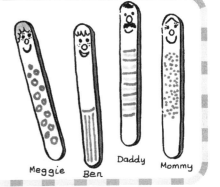

Meggie Ben Daddy Mommy

1. Direct children to take enough craft sticks to represent each member of their families.

2. Encourage children to decorate each craft stick to look like a different family member.

3. Help each child glue the craft sticks to his or her cardboard or poster board. Ask children to identify which family members they drew, then write each name below the appropriate stick.

PRESCHOOL CONNECTION

When children have finished, collect craft supplies. Read Genesis 1:26-27 aloud from an easy-to-understand Bible translation so children know the passage is in God's Word. Then ask:

· **How many people did God put in your family?**

· **Who in your family do you look like?**

· **Why do you think God made families?**

Say: **God made people, and he put us in families so we could be cared for by each other and learn to love each other the way God loves us. Because God made each of us, we're sort of like one big family! Let's give each of our brothers and sisters in this classroom a hug!** Lead children in hugging each other in a kind and loving way.

WOWS *that work*

Sing the following song to the tune of "This Old Man."

God loves you; God loves me.
God gave us a family.
Brothers, sisters, moms and daddies, too.
God is good to me and you!

ADAM AND EVE SIN
Genesis 3:1-24

What Kids Will Do: Sew two trees together and attach fruit stickers.

What Kids Will Need: green poster board, paper punch, yarn, tape, fruit or food stickers, scissors

Preparation Place: Cut out two simple tree shapes (approximately 6x9 inches) for each child. Stack two trees together and punch holes around the edge. Wrap a piece of tape to one end of the yarn to make a "needle."

EASY Steps   TREES OF LIFE

1. Give each child two trees and a long piece of yarn.

2. Encourage children to stack the trees together and then sew them with the yarn.

3. While children are sewing, remind them that God made trees and that God placed Adam and Eve in a garden with trees.

4. When children have completed their sewing projects, distribute fruit stickers and let children attach them to the trees.

Permission to photocopy this box from *The Encyclopedia of Bible Crafts for Preschoolers* granted for local church use.
Copyright © Group Publishing, Inc., P.O. Box 481, Loveland, CO 80539. www.grouppublishing.com

PRESCHOOL CONNECTION

When children have finished, collect craft supplies. Read Genesis 1:28-31 and Genesis 3:1-6 aloud from an easy-to-understand Bible translation so children know the passage is in God's Word. Then ask:

• **What did God give for Adam and Eve to eat?**

• **What rules did God give to Adam and Eve about what foods to eat?**

• **Why did the people disobey God?**

Say: **God gave his people lots and lots of food from which to choose. But God also had some rules to follow. Adam and Eve did not obey. So God had to punish them because they did not obey. You can hang this tree in your house to remind you to do what God says to do.**

WOWS that work

Let children tell some of the rules they must obey at home or at church. Each time a child says one rule, let children add another fruit sticker to their trees.

ADAM AND EVE SIN
Genesis 3:1-24

What Kids Will Do: Make paper people that "hide" like Adam and Eve.

What Kids Will Need: gingerbread cookie cutters, pencils or markers, construction paper, scissors, scraps of fabric, glue

Preparation Place: Set out all supplies on a table where children can reach them.

EASY Steps   HIDING FROM GOD

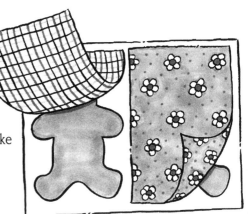

1. Give each child a sheet of paper, and write his or her name on the paper. Let children trace around the cookie cutters to make two people who represent Adam and Eve.

2. Help children cut pieces of fabric that are slightly bigger than the Adam and Eve figures.

3. Have children glue the top edge of each fabric scrap and place the fabric like a flap over each figure.

4. Allow the children to play Peekaboo with their figures by lifting the flaps.

PRESCHOOL CONNECTION

When children have finished, collect craft supplies. Read Genesis 3:6-10 aloud from an easy-to-understand Bible translation so children know the passage is in God's Word. Then ask:

- **Why were the people hiding?**
- **How do you feel when you've done something wrong?**
- **Why can't you hide from God?**

Say: **Adam and Eve had eaten the fruit God told them not to eat. They knew that was a wrong thing to do, so they felt bad. Then Adam and Eve made clothes to cover themselves, and they hid from God. We made our paper people and covered them to remind us of how Adam and Eve tried to hide from God. We can't hide from God! God loves us and wants us to come to him when we feel bad.**

that work

Have the children cover their eyes while you hide their paper people around the classroom. Encourage children to find their people, and remind them that *you* can't hide from God.

NOAH BUILDS AN ARK
Genesis 6:5–22

What Kids Will Do: Build arks to remember the boat that Noah built.

What Kids Will Need: Styrofoam meat trays, modeling dough, animal crackers, string or yarn

Preparation Place: Set out all supplies on a table where children can easily reach them.

EASY Steps

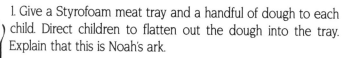

TWO BY TWO

1. Give a Styrofoam meat tray and a handful of dough to each child. Direct children to flatten out the dough into the tray. Explain that this is Noah's ark.

2. Let children look through the animal crackers to find matching pairs of animals.

3. Have the children set two or three pairs of animals in the dough in their ark.

4. Use a pencil to poke a hole in one edge of the ark and attach three feet of yarn or string to the boat. Let children sail their arks by pulling the string.

WOWS that work

Play a game to help the children practice doing what they're told to do. Have children gather near each other with their boats. Give children directions such as "Set your boats on the floor," "Walk around your boats," "Bend over and touch your boats," and "Sail your boats back over to the table."

PRESCHOOL CONNECTION

When children have finished, collect craft supplies. Read Genesis 6:5-22 aloud from an easy-to-understand translation of the Bible so children know the passage is in God's Word. Then ask:

• **Why did Noah build a boat or ark?**

• **What did God tell him to do with the animals?**

• **What kinds of animals do you have on your boat?**

Say: **Noah did what God told him to do. Even though it had never rained that hard before, Noah did what God said to do.** Ask:

• **When is it hard for you to do what you are told to do?**

Say: **God is pleased when we obey, like Noah. When you play with your boat, you can remember to obey God, even when it's hard.**

NOAH BUILDS AN ARK
Genesis 6:5-22

What Kids Will Do: Make rain hats from paper grocery sacks to remember that God sent rain to flood the earth.

What Kids Will Need: paper grocery sacks; glue; scissors; decorative items such as foam shapes, pompoms, string or yarn, fabric or wrapping paper scraps, or construction paper scraps

Preparation Place: Turn each sack inside out so the plain side is out. Roll the edges down so each sack is about half of its original size. You'll need one sack for each child.

EASY Steps · RAIN HATS

1. Set out the prepared grocery sack hats, and write each child's name on one. Show children how the bags can be turned over and worn as hats.

2. Direct children to decorate their rain hats, using the decorative items you've provided.

3. As children work, talk about what other clothes we wear when it rains.

4. When children finish, let them wear their hats!

PRESCHOOL CONNECTION

When children have finished, collect craft supplies. Open your Bible to Genesis 6:5-22, and show children the words. Tell the Bible story in your own preschool-friendly words. Then ask:

· **What happened after the animals all got on the ark?**

· **How did the people stay dry on Noah's ark?**

· **How do we stay warm and dry today?**

Say: **You all made rain hats to keep from getting wet in the rain. God sends rain to help flowers and plants grow. The rain also fills up our oceans, rivers, and lakes so we have good water to drink. I'm glad God provides rain for us! Let's put on our hats and praise God with a song.**

Lead children in singing the following song to the tune of "It's Raining, It's Pouring."

I'm praising, I'm praising!

'Cause God is amazing.

He gives us rain;

I can't complain.

Now my hands I'm raising!

that work

Children will look so cute in these hats that you might want to bring in an instant-print camera and take pictures. Give parents the pictures as a reminder of all that their children are learning about God!

NOAH BUILDS AN ARK
Genesis 6:5-22

What Kids Will Do: Make animal necklaces to show that God sent many animals to Noah's ark.

What Kids Will Need: foam animal shapes, colored drinking straws, 54-inch shoelaces, hole punch, scissors

Preparation Place: Cut each shoelace in half, and cut the straws into 2-inch lengths. For each child, tie one piece of drinking straw onto the end of a shoelace to keep the items from falling off the end. (You'll untie this and tie it to the other end of the lace after the children have completed their necklaces.) Then set all supplies where children can easily reach them.

EASY Steps — ANIMAL NECKLACES

1. Help children use a hole punch to make one hole in each animal shape.

2. Direct children to string a necklace by alternating the straw pieces with the foam shapes. (If children want to make their own unique patterns, that's OK too.)

3. Help children tie the ends together and wear their necklaces.

Permission to photocopy this box from *The Encyclopedia of Bible Crafts for Preschoolers* granted for local church use.
Copyright © Group Publishing, Inc., P.O. Box 481, Loveland, CO 80539. www.grouppublishing.com

PRESCHOOL CONNECTION

When children have finished, collect craft supplies. Read Genesis 6:5-22 aloud from an easy-to-understand translation of the Bible so children know the passage is in God's Word. Then ask:

· **What did you put on your necklace?**

· **What did Noah put on the ark?**

· **What do you think it was like to make all those animals get on the ark?**

Say: **Noah worked very hard to build the ark for all of the animals and his family. Noah made the ark just the way God said to. Then God helped Noah get everyone on the ark. When it stopped raining, God sent a rainbow for everyone to see. You can wear your necklace to remind you that God is watching over you and helping you.**

WOWS that work

While the people and animals lived on the ark, they had to work together and share everything. Encourage children to share their necklaces and give them to other people to wear.

THE ANIMALS CLIMB ABOARD

Genesis 7:1–16

What Kids Will Do: Create ark-shaped snack bags filled with animal shapes.

What Kids Will Need: brown paper lunch sacks, animal crackers, gummy bears, white address labels, black and brown markers

Preparation Place: Set out the supplies on a table where children can easily reach them.

EASY Steps   ANIMALS IN THE ARK

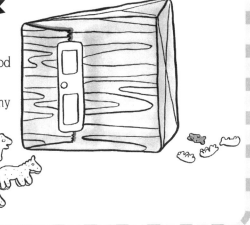

1. Give each child a paper sack, and write his or her name on it.

2. Encourage children to use markers to decorate their sacks to look like wood on the ark.

3. Ask the children to wash their hands and then fill their ark bags with gummy bears and animal crackers.

4. When the sacks are filled, ask the children to fold over the tops of their sacks and seal them with address labels. Encourage them to decorate the labels to look like the door of the ark.

PRESCHOOL CONNECTION

When children have finished, ask them to set their animal-filled arks in front of them. Read aloud Genesis 7:1-16 from an easy-to-understand Bible translation. Then ask:

- **How did Noah obey God?**
- **How do we obey God?**
- **Why does God want us to obey him?**

Say: **Noah obeyed God and built an ark. Noah filled the ark with animals so they'd be safe in the flood. We obey God when we love each other, listen to our parents, and tell others about him. God wants us to do what is right and always obey him.**

WOWS that work

Encourage kids to use their animal-filled arks to tell the story to their families when they go home.

THE ANIMALS CLIMB ABOARD
Genesis 7:1–16

What Kids Will Do: Design animal masks to remember some of the animals Noah brought on the ark.

What Kids Will Need: yellow and pink construction paper, feathers, yarn, paper plates, markers, glue, scissors

Preparation Place: Cut rectangular yellow strips for lions' manes and pink triangles for pigs' ears. Cut eyeholes in the paper plates, and attach an 8-inch piece of yarn to each side so children can tie on the masks. Set out all supplies on a table.

Easy Steps AMAZING ANIMAL MASKS

1. Give each child a paper plate. Let kids decide if they want to make a lion, pig, or bird mask.

2. Encourage children to glue feathers for bird masks, yellow strips for lions' manes, or pink triangles for pigs' ears.

3. Ask children to use the markers to add details to their masks.

4. When children finish, be sure each child's name is on the back of his or her mask. Help children tie the masks in place.

Permission to photocopy this box from *The Encyclopedia of Bible Crafts for Preschoolers* granted for local church use.
Copyright © Group Publishing, Inc., P.O. Box 481, Loveland, CO 80539. www.grouppublishing.com

PRESCHOOL CONNECTION

When children have finished, collect craft supplies. Read Genesis 7:1-16 aloud from an easy-to-understand Bible translation so children know the passage is in God's Word. Then ask:

· **How did Noah take care of the animals?**

· **Do you have a pet or know someone who has a pet? Or have you ever been to a zoo?**

· **How do people take care of animals?**

· **Why does God want us to take care of animals?**

Say: **Noah took care of the animals by building an ark to keep them safe when lots of rain would come. We take care of animals by brushing them and making sure they have food and water. God made the animals and wants us to take care of them.**

Let the children wear their masks and pretend they are the animals getting on board the ark. Gather them in a circle for a prayer. Let each child thank God for the animal his or her mask represents.

Set out a larger variety of supplies, such as glitter glue, felt squares, chenille wires, and cotton balls. Let the children design any kind of animal mask they want to—such as puppies, kittens, and sheep.

THE ANIMALS CLIMB ABOARD

Genesis 7:1-16

What Kids Will Do: Create clip-on characters of the Bible story.

What Kids Will Need: spring clothespins, Glue Dots, paper cups, crayons, craft foam people and animal shapes (You can find animal shapes and Glue Dots at most craft or hobby stores.)

Preparation Place: Set out all supplies on a table where children can easily reach and share.

EASY Steps   CLIP-ON CHARACTERS

1. Give four clothespins and a cup to each child, and ask kids to color the cups to look like Noah's ark.

2. Let the children use Glue Dots to attach people or animal shapes to their clothespins. Children should make one for Noah, one for a family member, and two for animals.

3. Show the children how to clip their characters onto their cup "arks."

Permission to photocopy this box from *The Encyclopedia of Bible Crafts for Preschoolers* granted for local church use.
Copyright © Group Publishing, Inc., P.O. Box 481, Loveland, CO 80539. www.grouppublishing.com

PRESCHOOL CONNECTION

When children have finished, collect craft supplies. Ask children to hold their crafts and sit in a circle. Have them remove their clothespin characters from their cups. Read Genesis 7:1-16 aloud from an easy-to-understand Bible translation so children know the passage is in God's Word. As you read, have the children clip on each character when that character boards the ark. Then ask:

· **How did Noah and his family work together in the story?**

· **What kinds of chores do you do to help your family?**

· **Why does God want us to work together at home?**

Say: **Noah and his family built the ark and then worked together to get the animals on board. We work together with our families when we do chores such as make our beds, set the table for dinner, and feed our pets. God wants us to work together and help each other, just as Noah and his family did.**

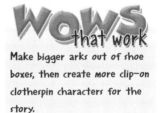

WOWS that work

Make bigger arks out of shoe boxes, then create more clip-on clothespin characters for the story.

19

THE BOAT BEGINS TO FLOAT
Genesis 7:17—8:13

What Kids Will Do: Make floating "arks" in bottles.

What Kids Will Need: clean, empty 2-liter plastic bottles; Styrofoam packing peanuts; water; blue food coloring; several pitchers or funnels; tarp if doing activity inside

Preparation Place: Plan to make these crafts outside, or place a large tarp on the floor.

EASY Steps   FLOATING BOATS

1. Give each child a bottle and Styrofoam peanut. Help the children fill their bottles half full with water.

2. Guide children as they squeeze ten drops of blue food coloring into the water, screw the cap back on the bottle, and shake the bottle so the water turns blue.

3. Ask the children to unscrew the cap, place the peanut inside, and then screw the cap back on.

4. Show kids how to turn the bottle on its side to watch the Styrofoam peanut boat float.

PRESCHOOL CONNECTION

When children have finished, collect craft supplies. Read Genesis 7:17–8:13 aloud from an easy-to-understand Bible translation so children know the passage is in God's Word. Then ask:

• **How did God keep Noah and the animals safe during the flood?**

• **When have you ever been on a boat? What did you think about floating on the water?**

• **How do you think Noah felt floating on a lot of water?**

Say: **God kept Noah and the animals safe in the ark. Sometimes it's fun to float on the water, but sometimes it can be scary—especially if we're riding on big waves. Noah and the animals must have had an exciting time riding on the water. They knew God loved them and kept them safe in the ark.**

Lead children in the following song, to the tune of "Row, Row, Row Your Boat."

Float, float, float along,

In the ark we go!

God takes care of all of us

For he loves us so!

THE BOAT BEGINS TO FLOAT
Genesis 7:17—8:13

What Kids Will Do: Make cupcake "doves" to remember how Noah found dry land.

What Kids Will Need: cupcakes, whipped topping, candy corns, Skittles candies, paper plates, spoon

Preparation Place: Spoon the whipped topping into a thin layer on a paper plate. Set the supplies on a table where children can easily reach and share. Have children wash their hands before preparing this snack.

EASY Steps   DELECTABLE DOVES

1. Give each child a cupcake on a paper plate.

2. Have children dip the top of the cupcake into the whipped topping, covering the top of the cupcake completely.

3. Encourage the children to use the candy corns to make beaks on their cupcake doves. Then let children add Skittles candies as eyes.

4. Children may eat the doves, or you may help children cover their plates with plastic wrap to take the doves home.

PRESCHOOL CONNECTION

When children have finished, collect craft supplies. Read Genesis 7:17—8:13 aloud from an easy-to-understand Bible translation so children know the passage is in God's Word. Then ask:

· **Have you ever been in a thunderstorm? How did you know when it was over?**

· **How did Noah know the flood was over? How do you think he felt?**

Say: **We know when a storm is over because the rain and wind stop. Noah knew the flood was over when the dove returned with a freshly plucked leaf! God used a special bird to help Noah be glad that the storm was over.**

GOD SENDS A RAINBOW
Genesis 9:8–16

What Kids Will Do: Create rainbows to remember God's promise to Noah.

What Kids Will Need: paper bowls, cotton balls, various colors of chenille wire, glue, green and brown tempera paint, paintbrushes, glue, smocks or old shirts, newspaper

Preparation Place: Cover a table with newspaper, and set out smocks or old shirts. Set all other supplies on the table where children can easily reach them.

THE FIRST RAINBOW

1. Give each child a bowl, four different colors of chenille wires, four cotton balls, and a paintbrush.

2. Ask children to turn their bowls upside down to be the earth. Let them paint the earth with the brown and green paint.

3. Once the paint dries, demonstrate how to stick the chenille wires into the bowl to form a rainbow. (Younger children may need help with this step.)

4. Encourage the children to glue two cotton balls to each end of the rainbow for clouds.

Permission to photocopy this box from *The Encyclopedia of Bible Crafts for Preschoolers* granted for local church use.
Copyright © Group Publishing, Inc., P.O. Box 481, Loveland, CO 80539. www.grouppublishing.com

PRESCHOOL CONNECTION

While children are waiting for the paint to dry on their crafts, gather them together. Read Genesis 9:8-16 aloud from an easy-to-understand Bible translation so children know the passage is in God's Word. Then ask:

• **How much longer do you think it'll be before the paint on our earth dries? Are you waiting patiently?**

• **How do you think Noah felt as he waited for the earth to dry so he could get off the ark?**

• **How do you think Noah felt when he saw the first rainbow?**

Say: **It must have been hard to be on the ark so long and wait for the earth to dry. When Noah and his family and the animals got off the ark, they saw a rainbow! The rainbow is a promise of love from God. Every time we see a rainbow, we can remember that God loves us.**

Let the kids finish their crafts by making rainbows from chenille wire and clouds from cotton balls.

For each wire that children stick into their bowls, have them say one way they know God loves them. Close in prayer, having kids tell God they love him, too.

GOD SENDS A RAINBOW
Genesis 9:8-16

What Kids Will Do: Make rainbow streamers and celebrate God's promises.

What Kids Will Need: drinking straws, tape, various colors of curling ribbon, scissors

Preparation Place: Cut ribbon into 18-inch pieces, and use the scissors to curl each piece. Make sure each child has six different colors. Set out the supplies on a table.

EASY Steps

CELEBRATION STREAMERS

1. Give each child a drinking straw and six different colors of ribbon. Place the children around the table so they can share the tape.

2. Encourage children to tape the various colors of ribbon to one end of a straw. Make sure each child makes one celebration streamer.

3. As the children work, affirm their efforts.

PRESCHOOL CONNECTION

Ask the children to bring their streamers and sit in a circle. Have them place their streamers in front of them. Read aloud the story of Noah and the rainbow from Genesis 9:8-16. Then ask:

- **What do you think Noah was thankful for?**
- **What are you thankful for?**
- **How do you show God you are thankful?**

Say: **Noah must have been thankful to be safe and on dry ground again. Then he saw such a beautiful rainbow and knew God loved him. We are thankful for so many things, such as families, food, church, and friends. We can tell God we are thankful by praising him in prayers and songs and by telling others about him.**

Go around the circle, and have each child say one thing he or she wants to thank God for. Encourage the children to wave their streamers high when each person shares.

Play upbeat music and lead children in a celebration parade. Move the streamers overhead, side to side, in a circle, and in wiggles. Every minute, stop the music and the parade. Let the kids shout, "Thank you, God!" Then start the music again.

GOD SENDS A RAINBOW

Genesis 9:8–16

What Kids Will Do: Make edible rainbows to remind them of God's promise to never again flood the earth.

What Kids Will Need: bowls of vanilla pudding, spoons, napkins, variety of colors of food coloring

Preparation Place: Set out all supplies where children can easily reach and share them.

EASY Steps

SCRUMPTIOUS RAINBOWS

1. Encourage the children to wash their hands and then gather around the table. Make sure each child has one bowl of pudding.

2. Have children tell you which colors of food coloring they'd like in their pudding. (Since food coloring can stain, it's best if an adult squeezes drops of the color for children.) Place several drops of different colors on one side of their vanilla pudding.

3. Show the children how to use their spoons and make each color into a part of a rainbow by moving the spoon from one side of the bowl to the other.

PRESCHOOL CONNECTION

When children have finished, collect craft supplies. Let the children eat their snacks while you read Genesis 9:8-16 aloud from an easy-to-understand Bible translation so children know the passage is in God's Word. Then ask:

- **What did God put in the sky as a promise to Noah?**
- **What does God promise us?**
- **How do you feel knowing God keeps all his promises?**

Say: **The rainbow is a promise that God will always love us. God promises to love us and forgive us. Because of Jesus, God promises that everyone who believes in him will live with him forever. God keeps his promises!**

THE PEOPLE BUILD A TALL TOWER
Genesis 11:1-9

What Kids Will Do: Build towers out of sandpaper squares.

What Kids Will Need: sandpaper, construction paper, pencils, glue, scissors

Preparation Place: Cut different grades of sandpaper into 1-inch squares. Cut enough squares so each child can have at least eight pieces. Set out construction paper and glue.

EASY Steps

TOWER BUILDERS

1. Gather the children around the supplies. Give each child at least eight sandpaper squares and one sheet of construction paper.

2. Encourage the children to glue the squares to the paper, like a tall tower.

3. Let children draw small people next to the tower to show how tall it is.

PRESCHOOL CONNECTION

When children have finished, collect craft supplies. Read Genesis 11:1-9 aloud from an easy-to-understand Bible translation so children know the passage is in God's Word. Then ask:

· **Who did the people in the story forget about?**

· **When do you sometimes forget about God?**

· **Where could you hang your picture to remind you that you always need God?**

Say: **The people in the story forgot about God. They tried to build a tall tower so they could make a name for themselves and be famous. Let's hang our pictures in our rooms at home. Every time you see your picture, remember that you always need God. He made you!**

Let the kids decorate their pages by coloring a frame around the edges. They could also use crayons to color the sandpaper squares.

THE PEOPLE BUILD A TALL TOWER
Genesis 11:1-9

What Kids Will Do: Spread liquid designs on handkerchiefs to show how God spread out the people.

What Kids Will Need: cotton handkerchiefs, eyedroppers, bowls, water, food coloring, newspaper

Preparation Place: Cover a table with newspaper. Spread out one handkerchief per child. Set out eyedroppers and bowls of food coloring mixed with water.

 **Steps**

SPREADING OUT

1. Give each child one handkerchief.

2. Encourage the children to share the eyedroppers and drop food coloring onto their handkerchiefs.

3. Tell them to notice how the food coloring soaks the cloth and spreads out.

4. Let the children design their cloths any way they want. Then let the handkerchiefs dry.

 **that work**

When the handkerchiefs dry, let the children wear them as scarves or ties. Encourage the children to tell people who comment on their colorful designs about how God spread the people out after they built a tall tower.

PRESCHOOL CONNECTION

While children are waiting for the handkerchiefs to dry, gather them together. Read Genesis 11:1-9 aloud from an easy-to-understand Bible translation so children know the passage is in God's Word. Then ask:

· **Why did the people want to build a tower?**

· **In the story, what happened because the people forgot they needed God?**

· **Why do we need God?**

Say: **The people believed they could do great things, so they built a tall tower. They forgot they needed God! So God mixed up their language and spread the people out. God wanted the people to learn that they needed him more than anything else.**

THE PEOPLE BUILD A TALL TOWER
Genesis 11:1–9

What Kids Will Do: Build edible brick towers to remind them of the tower of Babel.

What Kids Will Need: cornbread, knife, honey in squeeze bottles, paper plates, clean bed sheet

Preparation Place: Spread a clean sheet on the floor. Then cut cornbread into small, medium, and large squares so kids will be able to easily stack three. Set out the plates and squeeze bottles of honey.

EASY Steps — EDIBLE TOWERS

1. Encourage the children to wash their hands before they make their edible craft.

2. Ask the children to build towers on their plates, using large, medium, and small squares of cornbread.

3. Let the children pretend the honey is the mortar that holds the cornbread bricks together.

PRESCHOOL CONNECTION

Gather children on the sheet, and lead them in prayer, thanking God for all of his blessings. Then let children eat their cornbread towers. Read Genesis 11:1-9 aloud from an easy-to-understand Bible translation so children know the passage is in God's Word. Then ask:

· **Why did we build our towers?**

· **Why did the people build their tower?**

· **Who did the people in the story forget about?**

Say: **We built our towers because we wanted a snack. We remembered to pray to God and thank him for his blessings. The people in the story forgot all about God. They just wanted to build a tower so they could make a name for themselves and be famous. They acted as if they didn't need God at all. Let's always remember to thank God each and every day in all that we do.**

that work

Build bigger edible towers by using ready-made angel food cake rectangles (purchase these at grocery stores). Use frosting or whipped topping for the mortar between the bricks. If you build your edible towers on a bed sheet, it'll make cleaning up a snap!

GOD BLESSES ABRAM
Genesis 12:1-8

What Kids Will Do: Make map-designed bookmarks to remind them to follow God.

What Kids Will Need: poster board, old maps, glue, hole punch, curling ribbon, gel pens, scissors

Preparation Place: Cut bright colors of poster board into 2x6-inch strips. Cut old maps into 1x5-inch strips. Then cut curling ribbon into 10-inch pieces. Set out glue and gel pens.

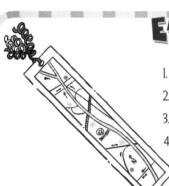

EASY Steps — MAP BOOKMARKS

1. Give each child one poster board strip and one map strip.

2. Encourage the children to share glue as they glue the map strips to their poster board strips.

3. Let the children decorate their bookmarks with gel pens.

4. Use a hole punch to make a hole in each bookmark. Let children thread curling ribbon through the hole. Tie the ribbon and curl it with scissors.

PRESCHOOL CONNECTION

When children have finished, collect craft supplies. Read Genesis 12:1-8 aloud from an easy-to-understand Bible translation so children know the passage is in God's Word. Then ask:

· **How do maps show us which way to go?**

· **How did Abram know which way to go?**

· **How does God show us how to live each day?**

Say: **Maps show us how to travel along roads, highways, cities, and states. Abram listened to God and followed the path God wanted him to take. In the Bible, God shows us how to live. Let's always read and listen to God's Word.**

WOWS that work

Make a map-designed bookmark for yourself, and place it in your Bible at Genesis 12:1-8. Before you read the story, hold up your bookmark and say: **Just as maps show us the way to go, God's Word—the Bible—shows us how to live each day.** Encourage kids to place their bookmarks in their Bibles or Bible story picture books at home and always remember to follow God.

GOD BLESSES ABRAM

Genesis 12:1–8

What Kids Will Do: Design silhouettes with ways God blesses them.

What Kids Will Need: butcher paper, markers, magazines, scissors, tape, glue, lamp with a strong light bulb

Preparation Place: Cut a sheet of butcher paper large enough for each child to have a silhouette from the shoulders on up. Set a lamp about 3 feet from a wall. Set out markers, magazines, scissors, and glue.

EASY Steps — GOD BLESSES ME, TOO

1. Tape a sheet of paper to a wall. Place a child in front of the paper, then a lamp in front of the child. The child should be standing so his or her silhouette is showing on the paper. Trace each child's silhouette. Let children cut out their silhouettes.

2. Ask the children to look through the magazines and find pictures of how God has blessed them, such as with fun friends, loving families, food, and clothing.

3. Tell the children to cut or tear out the photos and glue them to their silhouettes.

Permission to photocopy this box from *The Encyclopedia of Bible Crafts for Preschoolers* granted for local church use.
Copyright © Group Publishing, Inc., P.O. Box 481, Loveland, CO 80539. www.grouppublishing.com

PRESCHOOL CONNECTION

When children have finished, collect craft supplies. Read Genesis 12:1-8 aloud from an easy-to-understand Bible translation so children know the passage is in God's Word. Then ask:

· **How did God say he would bless Abram?**

· **How does God bless you?**

· **How can we thank God for all his blessings?**

Say: **God promised to bless Abram. Abram followed God and went to a new land that God said he would give him. God blesses us so much with food, families, clothes, and our church. We can thank God for his blessings by praying, singing, worshipping, and telling others about him.**

GOD BLESSES ABRAM
Genesis 12:1-8

What Kids Will Do: Make suitcases and pack things they would want to take on a trip.

What Kids Will Need: shoe boxes, stickers, glitter glue, markers, ribbon, bits of construction paper

Preparation Place: Set out all the supplies on a table.

EASY Steps   SUITCASES READY TO GO

1. Give each child a shoe box, then gather the kids around the supplies.

2. Encourage each child to decorate a shoe box "suitcase" with the supplies.

3. Ask kids to glue on designs and construction paper and color the box with markers. Ask them to draw things they would take with them if they went on a long trip, such as family members, books, toys, and food.

WOWS that work

Tell the children to take their shoe box suitcases home and fill them with reminders of things that are important to them—pictures of family, friends, or small items of things they like to do such as a baseball or a coloring book.

PRESCHOOL CONNECTION

Gather the children in a circle, then read aloud Genesis 12:1-8. Ask:

• **What do you think Abram took with him on his trip to a new land?**

• **If you had to move, what would you take with you on your trip?**

• **How can we trust that God loves us and wants the best for us no matter where we live?**

Say: **I think Abram took his family and things he really needed on his trip. I think he took clothes, food, water, and his pets and animals. If I had to move, I'd take the same things! No matter where we go, we can trust that God is with us and loves us!**

ISAAC IS COMING
Genesis 18:1-19; 21:1-7

What Kids Will Do: Design angel visitors to remind them of the story.

What Kids Will Need: 1-inch Styrofoam balls, cone-shaped paper cups, aluminum foil, tape, glue, black construction paper, hole punch, scissors

Preparation Place: Use the hole punch to make several holes from the construction paper. Cut the aluminum foil into 4-inch squares. Then set all the supplies on a table.

EASY Steps   ANGEL VISITORS

1. Give each child a cup and a Styrofoam ball. Let children use crayons to color their cups.

2. Let each child glue three black dots to his or her ball, creating eyes and a nose.

3. Ask the children to turn the cups upside down and then press the balls onto the tips of the "cones" and glue them in place.

4. Show children how to pinch the aluminum foil in the center to look like wings. Let them tape the wings to the cups.

PRESCHOOL CONNECTION

When children have finished, collect craft supplies. Read Genesis 18:1-19; 21:1-7 aloud from an easy-to-understand Bible translation so children know the passage is in God's Word. Then ask:

- **How do you think Abraham and Sarah felt when they saw the angels?**
- **How would you feel if you saw an angel?**
- **How will your craft help you remember the story?**

Say: **The angels promised that old Abraham and Sarah would have a son! I think Abraham and Sarah were surprised when they saw the angels, and they were happy that they would have a son. Keep your angels by your bed or on a table to remind you of the angels in our story.**

Kids will be gluing balls to the tips of cups to represent angels' heads and bodies. The balls will go on easier if you use the tip of scissors or a pen to make a hole in each ball prior to kids gluing them in place.

ISAAC IS COMING
Genesis 18:1–19; 21:1–7

What Kids Will Do: Create baby Isaacs as they learn that Abraham and Sarah had a baby named Isaac.

What Kids Will Need: table tennis balls, white handkerchiefs, blue ribbon, blue fabric pens, scissors

Preparation Place: Cut ribbon into 8-inch strips. Each child will need one table tennis ball, one handkerchief, and one piece of ribbon. Set the fabric pens on a table.

EASY Steps   BABY BUNDLES

1. Give each child one table tennis ball, one handkerchief, and one ribbon.

2. Show children how to place the ball in the center of the handkerchief and then gather the handkerchief tightly around it and secure it with the ribbon.

3. Explain that the ball is baby Isaac's head and the rest is his blanket. Let each child use a blue fabric pen to create a face for Isaac and designs on the blanket.

PRESCHOOL CONNECTION

When children have finished, collect craft supplies. Read Genesis 18:1–19; 21:1–7 aloud from an easy-to-understand Bible translation so children know the passage is in God's Word. Then ask:

• **How do you think Abraham and Sarah felt when God gave them baby Isaac?**

• **How do you think families feel when they receive a new baby?**

• **Besides babies, what other things does God give you that bring you joy?**

Say: **Sarah and Abraham must have felt so happy when God gave them baby Isaac. Babies bring such joy. God gives us so many things that make us happy, such as families who love us and places for us to live. The best blessing God gives us is his Son, Jesus, who loves us!**

Ask children to use their dolls to show you how people care for babies. Tell them that just as parents care for babies and love them, God cares for us and loves us.

A WIFE IS FOUND FOR ISAAC

Genesis 24

What Kids Will Do: Create Isaac and Rebekah paper dolls and attach their hands with magnets.

What Kids Will Need: construction paper, self-adhesive magnetic strips, crayons or washable markers, scissors

Preparation Place: For each child, cut out two 8-inch people shapes from construction paper. (The shapes should appear to have on robes.) Set out all other supplies where children can easily reach them.

EASY Steps   ISAAC AND REBEKAH

1. Give each child two paper people.

2. Explain that one doll is Isaac and one is Rebekah. Let children use the crayons or markers to decorate each paper doll.

3. Help children attach the magnetic strips to Isaac's left hand and Rebekah's right hand. When the magnets meet, it looks like the couple is holding hands.

PRESCHOOL CONNECTION

When children have finished, collect craft supplies. Open your Bible to Genesis 24, and show children the words so they will know the passage is in God's Word. Then tell the story of Isaac and Rebekah in your own preschool-friendly words. Ask:

• **How did the servant in the story ask God for help in finding Isaac a wife?**

• **When do you pray?**

• **Why does God want us to pray?**

Say: **The servant in the story prayed to God and asked for help in finding Isaac a wife. God answered his prayers and helped find Rebekah for Isaac's wife. Let's pray always and ask God for help, no matter what we face in life.**

Lead children in prayer, asking God to help them in all of life's challenges.

A WIFE IS FOUND FOR ISAAC
Genesis 24

What Kids Will Do: Create game pages with spinners and see how we can seek God's direction.

What Kids Will Need: photocopies of "God's Directions" (p. 35), metal paper fasteners, markers, scissors

Preparation Place: Photocopy a game and spinner (on p. 35) for each child. Set out all other supplies where children can easily reach them.

EASY Steps   FOLLOW GOD'S DIRECTIONS

1. Give each child a game page and a metal paper fastener.

2. Let each child cut out his or her game and spinner. Younger preschoolers might need help with this step.

3. Children may use markers to decorate their game boards.

4. Help each child use a metal paper fastener to attach the spinner to the center of the game board.

WOWS that work

Let the children take turns moving the spinners on their game boards. When the spinner lands on a section, ask the children to say how they can ask for God's help in that way for something in their lives. For example, if the spinner points to the child praying, kids could tell you something they want to pray for. Or if the spinner points to the child worshipping, kids could tell you something they want to thank God for.

PRESCHOOL CONNECTION

When children have finished, collect craft supplies. Open your Bible to Genesis 24, and show children the words so they will know the passage is in God's Word. Then tell the story of Isaac and Rebekah in your own preschool-friendly words. Ask:

· **How did God give Isaac direction in the story?**

· **How can we look for God's direction or help in life?**

· **Why should we look for God's direction?**

Say: **God gave direction by using Isaac's dad and his servant to help Isaac find a wife. The servant prayed and asked for God's direction too. These game boards will help you discover lots of ways to find God's direction.** Move the spinner, and ask the children to describe each picture to which the arrow points: a child reading or looking at pictures in the Bible; a child listening to a caring, Christian adult; a child worshipping; and a child praying. **God always wants us to follow his direction in life. God knows what's best for us.**

GOD'S DIRECTIONS

JACOB DECEIVES ESAU AND ISAAC
Genesis 25:19-34; 27:1-40

What Kids Will Do: Prepare Jacob and Esau puppets to tell the story.

What Kids Will Need: round lollipops (such as Tootsie Pops), wire twist ties, 6-inch squares of felt, tissues, markers

Preparation Place: Set all the supplies on a table where children can easily reach and share them.

EASY Steps   LOLLIPOP PUPPETS

1. Give each child two lollipops.

2. Let each child cover one lollipop with a felt square and then secure it under the candy with a twist tie. He or she should cover the other sucker with both tissues and then secure them with another twist tie.

3. Direct children to use markers to make a simple face on each puppet—one for Jacob and one for Esau.

PRESCHOOL CONNECTION

When children have finished, collect craft supplies. Ask the children to bring their puppets and sit down in a circle. Read Genesis 25:19-34; 27:1-40 aloud from an easy-to-understand Bible translation so children know the passage is in God's Word. Then ask:

· **Why do you think Jacob lied in the story?**

· **When is it hard to tell the truth? Why?**

· **Why does God want us to tell the truth?**

Say: **Jacob had to run away because he told a lie. He hurt his brother and made his whole family sad. So much sadness was caused because of a lie. God wants us to tell the truth!**

Form pairs, and have children use their puppets to retell the story. Have them feel the different fabric on their puppets when blind Isaac is trying to tell his sons apart.

JACOB DECEIVES ESAU AND ISAAC
Genesis 25:19-34; 27:1-40

What Kids Will Do: Cover one of their gloves with fur and keep their second gloves plain, then retell the story.

What Kids Will Need: pairs of knit gloves, fake fur, glue, scissors

Preparation Place: Cut fake fur into smaller strips the kids can glue to gloves. Set the rest of the supplies on a table.

EASY Steps

HAIR YOU GO

1. Give each child a pair of gloves.

2. Have the children keep one glove plain and glue fake fur to the other glove.

3. Let the glue dry, and write kids names on their gloves.

PRESCHOOL CONNECTION

When children have finished, collect craft supplies. Ask the children to bring their puppets and sit down in a circle. Read Genesis 25:19-34; 27:1-40 aloud from an easy-to-understand Bible translation so children know the passage is in God's Word. When you first describe Jacob, have kids feel the plain glove. When you first describe Esau, have the kids feel the hairy glove. When you tell how Jacob dressed like his brother, have kids feel the hairy glove again. Then ask:

· **Why do you think it was wrong that Jacob pretended to be his brother?**

· **Why does God want us to tell the truth?**

· **When is it hard for you to tell the truth?**

Say: **Jacob pretended to be his brother so he could steal his brother's money and property. It's wrong to tell lies. People get hurt! Place your gloves where you can see them each day. Remember to always tell the truth!**

WOWS that work

Ask the kids to wear the gloves and retell the story— the plain glove for Jacob and the hairy glove for Esau. When they get to the part where Jacob dresses like Esau, have them hold the hairy glove high and say, "Jacob dressed like Esau and fooled his dad. That was wrong. Always tell the truth!" Remind the children that later Jacob was very sorry for what he did. God forgave him, and so did his brother.

JOSEPH TELLS HIS DREAMS
Genesis 37:1-11

What Kids Will Do: Make star sandwiches to remember the stars in Joseph's dream.

What Kids Will Need: sliced white bread, sliced wheat bread, star cookie cutters, plastic knives, grape jam, napkins

Preparation Place: Set out all items on a clean table where children can easily reach them. Be sure to have children wash their hands before preparing this craft snack.

EASY Steps — STAR SANDWICHES

1. Give each child a slice of white bread and a slice of wheat bread.

2. Have children cut one or two star shapes from each slice.

3. Show children how to use the white stars to fill in the star spaces on the wheat slice. Do the same with the wheat stars (like a jigsaw puzzle).

4. Help children use plastic knives to spread grape jam on the bread. Put the two slices together for a sandwich.

PRESCHOOL CONNECTION

As the children eat their sandwiches, read Genesis 37:1-11 aloud from an easy-to-understand Bible translation. Then ask:

· **How do you think Joseph's brothers felt when he told them about his dream about the stars? Why?**

· **Why do you think God is unhappy when families don't get along?**

· **What are some good ways to treat your family members?**

Say: **Joseph's brothers hated him because they didn't understand his dreams. They did not show love for their brother Joseph. God gave us our families and wants brothers and sisters to love each other.**

Lead the children in a prayer, asking God to help them get along with their brothers and sisters and to show love.

JOSEPH TELLS HIS DREAMS

Genesis 37:1–11

What Kids Will Do: Make Bendy Brothers so they can act out Joseph's brothers bowing down.

What Kids Will Need: brown construction paper, scissors, crayons, wire twist ties or chenille wires, wide tape

Preparation Place: Trace several simple gingerbread man shapes on brown paper. If you're using chenille wires, cut them into 4-inch pieces.

EASY Steps — BENDY BROTHERS

 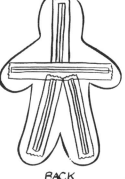

FRONT   BACK

1. Give each child a sheet of paper with a gingerbread man shape on it. Help children cut out the people shapes.

2. Let children draw faces and clothes on one side of their "people."

3. Show children how to tape the twist ties to the back of the person, on the legs, arms, and head.

4. Direct children to bend their men to look as if they are bowing down.

PRESCHOOL CONNECTION

When the children have finished, collect the craft supplies. Read Genesis 37:1-11 aloud from the Bible so the children know the passage is in God's Word. Then ask:

• **Why do you think Joseph's brothers were angry?**

• **How would you feel if someone told you a dream like Joseph's?**

• **Who do you think gave Joseph his dreams?**

Say: **Joseph's dreams told about something that would happen in the future. His brothers did not understand the meaning of Joseph's dreams. They didn't know that Joseph was being obedient to God and that it was God who sent the dreams. Joseph obeyed God and always followed God's ways. God wants us to be obedient too.**

Let children take turns standing up and shouting, "I'll obey God!"

JOSEPH IS SOLD INTO SLAVERY
Genesis 37:12-36

What Kids Will Do: Make cheerful butterfly finger puppets to remind them to be cheerful even during hard times.

What Kids Will Need: old knit gloves, 2-inch chenille wires, 4x4-inch pieces of construction paper, moveable eyes, stickers, markers, craft glue, scissors

Preparation Place: Cut the fingers from old gloves so there's one finger for each child.

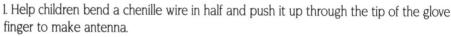

CHEERFUL BUTTERFLY FINGER PUPPETS

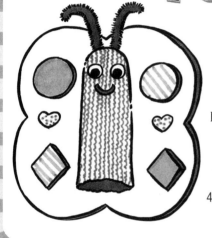

1. Help children bend a chenille wire in half and push it up through the tip of the glove finger to make antenna.

2. Guide children as they each cut a set of butterfly wings from the construction paper. Help them glue the glove finger to the center of the wings.

3. Let children glue two wiggly eyes to the top of the finger. (If you are working with very small children, substitute paper circles for eyes.) Children may add stickers to the wings for details.

4. Allow children to use markers to draw mouths on their butterflies.

PRESCHOOL CONNECTION

Leave the butterflies on the table to dry as you gather the children in a circle. Read Genesis 37:12-36 aloud from the Bible so the children know the passage is in God's Word. Then ask:

· **How can you tell when someone is frightened or sad?**

· **What do you do when you are frightened?**

· **How do you think Joseph felt when he was alone in the pit?**

Say: **Joseph must have been very frightened and sad when his brothers put him in that pit. But Joseph knew God would take care of him, and that made him cheerful. We can be cheerful, too, because we know God will take care of us.**

Go around the circle, and have each child say, "Thank you, God, for making us cheerful!"

You can find inexpensive knit gloves at many secondhand or thrift stores.

JOSEPH IS SOLD INTO SLAVERY
Genesis 37:12-36

What Kids Will Do: Make paper bag buddies as reminders that God is always with us.

What Kids Will Need: paper lunch sacks, newspaper, 1x9-inch strips of construction paper, yarn, markers, glue, large box

Preparation Place: Set all the supplies on the floor so children have plenty of room to work.

EASY Steps   JOSEPH BAG BUDDIES

1. Let each child crumple newspaper and use it to fill one bag. Help each child slide a second bag over the open "mouth" of the first bag. Glue the edges of the second bag to the first bag.

2. To define the head of the bag buddy, help children tie a 12-inch length of yarn tightly around the bags, about one third of the way down from the top.

3. Show children how to accordion-fold four 1x9-inch strips of construction paper and glue the strips to the bag to create arms and legs.

4. Children may use markers to draw a face and clothes on the bag.

PRESCHOOL CONNECTION

Clean up the craft materials, and set the Joseph Bag Buddies in a row. Read Genesis 37:12-36 aloud from an easy-to-understand Bible translation so the children know the passage is in God's Word. Then ask:

· **Have you ever had to wait for something to happen?**

· **How did you feel while you were waiting?**

· **What does it mean to be patient?**

· **How do you think being patient can please God?**

Say: **Joseph's brothers were jealous of him, so they threw him in a deep, dark pit. Joseph didn't know what was going to happen to him. He had to be patient and trust God to take care of him. God took care of Joseph, and God will take care of us, too. You can use your Joseph Bag Buddy to remind you that God is always beside you.**

Provide a large box to use as the pit. Let the children role-play the story by placing their Joseph Bag Buddies in the box. Remind children that God was with Joseph, even when Joseph felt all alone.

JOSEPH IS SOLD INTO SLAVERY
Genesis 37:12-36

What Kids Will Do: Make Family Photo Albums to show how much they love their family members.

What Kids Will Need: sheets of 9x12-inch construction paper, sheets of 8½x11-inch white paper, glue sticks, 3-hole punch, 12-inch pieces of ribbon, crayons or markers

Preparation Place: Before children arrive, use a 3-hole punch to make holes along one edge of the sheets of construction paper. Set out all supplies where children can reach them.

EASY Steps

FAMILY PHOTO ALBUMS

1. Give each child six sheets of white paper and six sheets of construction paper. Have children glue a sheet of white paper to the center of each sheet of construction paper.

2. Show children how to stack the papers together so the holes line up on the left side. Let children weave ribbon through the holes, and help them tie the ribbons securely.

3. Allow children to draw pictures of their families on the pages of their "books."

4. Write, "My Family Album" on the cover sheet, along with each child's name.

PRESCHOOL CONNECTION

When the children finish, clean up the craft area. Read Genesis 37:12-36 aloud from an easy-to-understand translation of the Bible. Then ask:

- **Who are the members of your family?**
- **How do you act when your brother or sister makes you angry?**
- **What did Joseph's brothers do when they were angry?**
- **How do you think God wants us to treat our family members?**

Say: **God gave us families to love and to work together. Joseph's brothers did a bad thing when they were angry with Joseph. They were jealous. God is not happy when we are jealous. God wants us to be loving and kind to the people in our families.**

Lead the children in a prayer, asking God to help them treat family members with love and kindness.

WOWS that work

Take a picture of your class so each child can add a picture of the *church family* to his or her album.

JOSEPH FORGIVES HIS BROTHERS

Genesis 42:1–45:28

What Kids Will Do: Use cereal to make pictures of Joseph's family.

What Kids Will Need: paper plates, oat ring cereal, puffed rice cereal, wheat stalks, raffia, craft glue, marker, hole punch

Preparation Place: Before children arrive, punch two holes, about 2 inches apart, at the top of each plate. Set all other supplies on a table where children can reach them.

EASY Steps

WHOLE GRAIN FAMILY

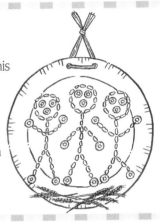

1. Allow each child to draw three stick figure men on a paper plate to represent Joseph and his brothers.

2. Help children glue puffed rice to the plate, outlining the figures.

3. Let children glue oat ring cereal to the figures as hands, feet, eyes, and mouths.

4. Have children glue a few stalks of wheat to the bottom of the paper plate. Then children may slip raffia through the holes at the top. Tie off the raffia to make a door hanger.

PRESCHOOL CONNECTION

Clean up the craft supplies. Open your Bible to Genesis 42:1–45:28. Use your own preschool-friendly words to summarize the story. Then ask:

- **When do you feel hungry?**
- **Where do you go to find food?**
- **Where did Joseph's family go to find food?**
- **Who provides food for you?**

Say: **Joseph's family was very hungry because they couldn't grow any crops or grain. They went to Egypt to buy grain, and there they found the brother they had sold into slavery. Instead of being angry, Joseph forgave his brothers. Now his family was together again! God likes it when families forgive each other!**

Let the children take turns praying, thanking God for each family member by name.

To keep little fingers cleaner, you might let children use cotton swabs to apply the glue to the stick figures. Then all the children have to do is lay the cereal pieces in place.

JOSEPH FORGIVES HIS BROTHERS
Genesis 42:1–45:28

What Kids Will Do: Make heart baskets as symbols of forgiveness.

What Kids Will Need: pink or red construction paper, yarn, stickers, hole punch, scissors, marker, adhesive bandages

Preparation Place: Trace two large hearts for each child on construction paper. Cut yarn into 2-foot lengths, and wrap a strip of tape around one end of each length.

EASY Steps   FORGIVING HEART BASKETS

1. Give each child two sheets of construction paper (with a heart drawn on each one), and let children cut along the lines to make two hearts.

2. Help children stack the hearts, and punch holes along the outside edges.

3. Guide children as they sew in and out the holes with yarn, leaving a length of yarn at the top for a handle.

4. Allow children to decorate the outside of the heart with stickers.

PRESCHOOL CONNECTION

Clean up the craft supplies. Open your Bible to Genesis 42:1–45:28. Use your own preschool-friendly words to summarize the story. Then ask:

· **How do you feel when someone hurts you?**

· **What do you do to that person who has hurt you?**

· **How do you think God wants us to treat that person?**

Say: **Joseph could have hated his brothers for being so mean, but instead he forgave them. Joseph had a forgiving heart. God wants us to have forgiving hearts too. Joseph's actions pleased God. God is pleased with us when we are forgiving.**

Give each child an adhesive bandage to place in his or her heart craft. Explain that the bandages will remind kids to forgive with their whole hearts, even when people hurt them.

WOWS that work

Encourage the children to put flowers or treats in their baskets and give them to people who they need to ask for forgiveness.

JOSEPH FORGIVES HIS BROTHERS

Genesis 42:1—45:28

What Kids Will Do: Make rulers' rings like Joseph might have worn.

What Kids Will Need: craft foam, chenille wire, craft glue, glitter, newspaper, scissors

Preparation Place: Cover a table with newspaper to catch excess glitter. Cut 1-inch circles and diamonds from craft foam, then cut chenille wires into 3-inch pieces. Set all supplies on the table where children can reach them.

EASY Steps   RULERS' RINGS

1. Let each child select a craft foam shape for his or her ring.

2. Help children poke one end of a chenille wire up through the center of the foam and then back down.

3. Help children wrap the two ends of wire together, pinching the ends securely to avoid sharp edges.

4. Have children spread glue on the foam piece and sprinkle it with glitter.

PRESCHOOL CONNECTION

Clean up the supplies, and leave the rings on the table to dry. Hold the Bible open to Genesis 42:1—45:28 as you tell today's story in your own words. Then ask:

- **What does a king or ruler do?**
- **How do you act when you're around someone important?**
- **How do you think Joseph's brothers felt when they found out he was a ruler?**

Say: **Joseph's brothers thought he was dead, but God brought Joseph to Egypt and made him a great ruler so he could help his family. Joseph forgave his brothers because he loved them. God forgives us when we do wrong because God loves us.**

WOWS *that work*

Use a towel or cloth to make a royal cape. Let children wear their rings and play the role of Joseph talking to his brothers.

EXODUS

GOD KEEPS BABY MOSES SAFE
Exodus 1:1–2:10

What Kids Will Do: Make Moses in his basket.

What Kids Will Need: small paper plates, 30-inch pieces of yarn, green tissue paper, wooden clothespins, 4-inch cloth squares, crayons, fine-tipped marker, hole punch, paper shredder, scissors

Preparation Place: Put several sheets of green tissue paper through a shredder to make "grass." Cut the paper plates in half, hold the rims together and use the hole punch to make holes around the rim.

Easy Steps   BABY IN A BASKET

1. Give each child two paper plate halves, and let children color the outsides of the paper plates brown. Help children line up the holes and sew around the edges with yarn to make baskets.

2. Let children drizzle glue on the insides of their baskets and stuff them with shredded green tissue paper.

3. Help each child use a fine-tipped marker to draw a simple face on the head of his or her clothespin. Children may wrap the clothespin in the square of cloth and glue the ends of the cloth together.

4. Direct children to put "baby Moses" in the basket.

PRESCHOOL CONNECTION

Put the craft supplies away, and let the children hold their baskets and babies as you read Exodus 1:1–2:10 from a preschool-friendly Bible translation. Then ask:

• **Who took care of you when you were a baby?**

• **Who takes care of you now?**

Say: **The wicked Pharaoh wanted to kill all the baby boys. Moses' mother did not want her baby hurt, so she put him in a basket and hid him in the river. God saw Moses and provided a way for him to be safe. Moses' mother loved him very much. God loved Moses very much. God took care of Moses, and God will take care of us, too, because God loves us.**

Teach the children a simple lullaby that they can sing as they rock their babies.

GOD KEEPS BABY MOSES SAFE

Exodus 1:1–2:10

What Kids Will Do: Make regal crowns to remind them of the princess who found Moses.

What Kids Will Need: 11x22-inch sheets of construction paper (in a variety of colors), gel markers, metallic paper, stickers, jewels, glue, stapler, scissors

Preparation Place: Cut the construction paper into 3x22-inch strips. Set all other supplies on a table where children can easily reach them.

EASY Steps — CROWNS OF COMPASSION

1. Give each child a strip of paper. Explain that the strips of paper are going to be simple crowns. Write each child's name on the back of his or her crown.

2. Let children use stickers, scraps of shiny paper, gel markers, and plastic jewels to decorate their crowns.

3. Wrap each child's crown around his or her head so it fits snugly. Remove the crown and staple it at the correct size.

PRESCHOOL CONNECTION

Put away the craft supplies, and let the children wear their crowns as you read aloud Exodus 1:1–2:10 from an easy-to-understand Bible translation. Then ask:

- **What are princesses like?**
- **Why do you think the princess wanted to keep baby Moses?**
- **What might have happened if the princess hadn't found Moses?**

Say: **Moses' life was in danger, so he couldn't stay with his mother. God sent Moses to a princess who wanted to care for the baby. The princess took care of baby Moses so that he was safe. God sends people to care for us, too. God always provides what we need.**

Lead the children in the following rhyming prayer, thanking God for providing all we need.

Dear God,

All I need

Comes from you.

Thank you, God!

Your love is true.

In Jesus' name, amen.

Obtain baby pictures of your students ahead of time from parents, and display them on a bulletin board. Let the children guess who is in each picture.

GOD KEEPS BABY MOSES SAFE
Exodus 1:1–2:10

What Kids Will Do: Make hanging hearts from paper doilies, showing all the people who loved baby Moses.

What Kids Will Need: small heart-shaped doilies, large heart-shaped doilies, pink construction paper, 24-inch lengths of pink ribbon, scissors, glue, marker, child-safe scissors

Preparation Place: Trace four heart shapes on each sheet of pink construction paper. One heart should be slightly larger than the large doily, and three hearts should be slightly larger than the small doilies. Tie a loop at one end of each ribbon.

EASY Steps

HANGING HEARTS

1. Give each child a sheet of pink construction paper and a pair of child-safe scissors. Help children cut out the hearts.

2. Let children glue the doily hearts to the construction paper hearts.

3. Allow children to glue their large hearts to one end of their ribbons, leaving the loops at the top. Children should glue the three small hearts at 2-inch intervals down the ribbon.

4. Write, "God" on the large heart. Write, "Moses' Mother," "Miriam," and "The Princess" on the three small hearts.

PRESCHOOL CONNECTION

Clean up the craft supplies. Leave the hanging hearts on the table to dry as you read aloud Exodus 1:1–2:10 from an easy-to-understand Bible translation. Then ask:

- **What could you do to keep a baby safe in your house?**
- **What makes you feel safe?**
- **How do you think God keeps us safe?**

Say: **Moses was just a baby when Pharaoh wanted to kill him. God sent people to keep him safe. Moses' mother kept her son safe by making a basket to put him in. Moses' sister, Miriam, kept Moses safe by watching him. The princess kept Moses safe by taking him home and raising him in the palace as her son. Each person loved Moses and helped God keep him safe. God uses people like our parents to keep us safe too.**

Have children say, "Thank you, God, for keeping me safe today!"

WOWS that work

Take a walk around the room, and identify things that might not be safe for a baby if one came to visit your classroom. Discuss how the children could help keep the baby safe.

MOSES MEETS GOD AT THE BURNING BUSH
Exodus 2:11—3:20

What Kids Will Do: Make Moses figures that move toward burning bushes.

What Kids Will Need: construction paper, magnetic strips, red and yellow tissue paper, cotton balls, glue, photocopies of "Moses" (p. 50), crayons, scissors

Preparation Place: Make a photocopy of the "Moses" figure on page 50 for each child. Cut construction paper into 6x8-inch sheets. Cut tissue paper into 2-inch squares.

EASY Steps   MAGNETIC MOSES

1. Give each child a sheet of construction paper. Let children glue two cotton balls at the top for clouds and then stretch out the cotton so it covers the top of the paper.

2. Let children crumple and glue the tissue paper squares to the right side of the paper, forming the shape of a bush.

3. Help children glue a 4-inch piece of magnetic strip to the center back of the picture. Direct children to color and cut out their pictures of Moses and then glue ¹/₂-inch pieces of magnetic strip to his back.

4. Show children how to set Moses on the front of the picture with his magnet connecting to the one on the back of the picture. Children can move Moses toward the burning bush.

MAGNET ON BACK

PRESCHOOL CONNECTION

Clean up the craft supplies, and open your Bible to Exodus 2:11–3:20. Tell the Bible story in your own preschool-friendly words. Then ask:

- **What is the most unusual thing you have ever seen?**
- **What would you do if you saw a burning bush?**
- **How do you think Moses felt when he heard God's voice coming from the bush?**

Say: **When Moses saw the burning bush, he was curious and wanted a closer look. But God called to him and told him to stop because he was on holy ground—that means it was a special place because God was there. Moses listened to God. We can listen to God when we listen to the Bible. God is pleased when we listen to him.**

WOWS that work

As you tell the story, let children take their shoes off, just as Moses did.

49

MOSES

MOSES MEETS GOD AT THE BURNING BUSH

Exodus 2:11—3:20

What Kids Will Do: Sponge paint burning bushes like the one Moses saw.

What Kids Will Need: 8x9-inch pieces of poster board; markers; paint shirts; red, yellow, and orange tempera paint; 1-inch squares of sponge; spring clothespins; paper plate; newspaper

Preparation Place: Cover a table with newspaper to protect your work area. Pour small amounts of red, yellow, and orange paint on a paper plate.

EASY Steps   BURNING BUSHES

1. Give each child a sheet of poster board, and allow him or her to draw an outline of a bush. Then help children put on paint shirts.

2. Let each child pinch a sponge square in a clothespin. Show children how to dab the sponge in the paint and then onto the bush shape. (Encourage children to blot or stamp rather than brush the paint.)

3. Allow children to work until their bushes are covered with "fire."

Permission to photocopy this box from *The Encyclopedia of Bible Crafts for Preschoolers* granted for local church use.
Copyright © Group Publishing, Inc. P.O. Box 481, Loveland, CO 80539. www.grouppublishing.com

PRESCHOOL CONNECTION

Clean up the craft supplies, and leave the bushes on the table to dry. Open your Bible to Exodus 2:11–3:20. Tell the story of Moses and the burning bush, using your own preschool-friendly words. Then ask:

- **What kinds of things frighten you?**
- **Who do you go to when you are afraid?**
- **How does God take care of us?**

Say: **Moses heard God's voice speaking to him from a burning bush. God told Moses to go to Egypt and tell Pharaoh to free God's people. Moses was afraid, but God said he would help Moses. It was not an easy job for Moses to do, but God was with him. God is with us, too.**

To make a "burning bush" in your classroom, bring in a small fake bush with lots of branches. (Even some dead, dry branches will work fine.) Help children wind pieces of red, yellow, and orange yarn to the branches. Then turn on a fan and watch the "flames" dance!

MOSES MEETS GOD AT THE BURNING BUSH

Exodus 2:11–3:20

What Kids Will Do: Make sheep to remember that Moses was watching his sheep when he saw the burning bush.

What Kids Will Need: large craft sticks, wooden spring clothespins, black markers, wiggly eyes, cotton balls, glue

Preparation Place: Set out supplies on a table so children can easily reach them.

EASY Steps — MOSES' SHEEP

1. Give each child a craft stick, and instruct children to color an inch on the end of the craft stick (both sides) with black markers. Then let each child glue a wiggly eye to each side of the black section of the stick. (Or use construction paper circles for very small children.) This makes the sheep's face.

2. With the black "face" pointing left, let each child clip two clothespins to the craft stick, about 2 inches apart. Children may color the ends of the clothespins black to make the sheep's feet.

3. Help children smear their craft sticks and clothespins with glue and then attach cotton balls all over.

Permission to photocopy this box from *The Encyclopedia of Bible Crafts for Preschoolers* granted for local church use.
Copyright © Group Publishing, Inc., P.O. Box 481, Loveland, CO 80539. www.grouppublishing.com

PRESCHOOL CONNECTION

Clean up the craft supplies. Leave the sheep on the table to dry while you open your Bible to Exodus 2:11–3:20 and summarize the story of Moses and the burning bush. Then ask:

- **What jobs or chores do you do at your house?**
- **What special jobs can you do for God?**

Say: **Moses' job was taking care of sheep. One day God spoke to him from a burning bush and gave him a special job to do. Moses left his job of tending sheep and did what God asked. God was pleased because Moses was obedient. We, too, can please God by obeying.**

Close with this simple rhyming prayer:

Dear God,

Help me to obey you

In all I say and do.

Guide my words (place your hand to your mouth),

My hands (wiggle your fingers),

My feet. (Wiggle feet.)

And help me follow you.

In Jesus' name, amen.

MOSES PLEADS WITH PHARAOH

Exodus 7:14–12:30

What Kids Will Do: Make glittering frog bookmarks to remember the plague of frogs sent by God.

What Kids Will Need: clear adhesive paper, green glitter, 8-inch lengths of ribbon, scissors, glue, newspaper, permanent marker

Preparation Place: Cover a table with newspaper to help catch extra glitter. Use a permanent marker to draw a simple frog shape on one end of a 3x6-inch sheet of clear adhesive paper for each child. (See bottom of page for frog shape.) Set all other supplies within easy reach of children.

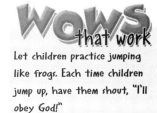

Let children practice jumping like frogs. Each time children jump up, have them shout, "I'll obey God!"

GLITTERING FROG BOOKMARKS

1. Help children peel away the backing on the adhesive papers and lightly sprinkle half of the sticky area with green glitter.

2. Let children fold their papers so the top and bottom meet with the sticky sides together. Have children smooth out any bumps or bubbles.

2. Guide children in cutting around their frog shapes.

3. Allow children to glue their frogs to one end of their ribbons.

PRESCHOOL CONNECTION

Clean up the craft supplies. Let the bookmarks dry on the table as you read Exodus 7:14–12:30 from an age-appropriate picture Bible. Then ask:

• **Have you ever asked someone to do something for you?**

• **How would you feel if that person promised to do it and then changed his or her mind?**

• **How do you think God feels when we break a promise to him?**

Say: **God covered Egypt with frogs because Pharaoh would not let God's people go. God is sad when we choose to disobey. But when we look inside God's Word—the Bible—and obey what it says, God is so happy. You can use your bookmark to mark special pages in your picture Bible at home!**

MOSES PLEADS WITH PHARAOH
Exodus 7:14–12:30

What Kids Will Do: Make locust reminders of the plague of locusts.

What Kids Will Need: green construction paper; chenille wires; small, green pom-poms; wiggly eyes; craft glue; hole punch; glue or stapler

Preparation Place: Roll 3-inch sheets of green construction paper into tubes, gluing or stapling the seam closed. You'll need one tube for each child.

EASY Steps   LIVELY LOCUSTS

1. Give each child a green tube, and help him or her punch three holes on each side of the tube opposite each other.

2. Let each child thread an 8-inch piece of chenille wire through two holes opposite each other.

3. Show children how to bend the wire down and then out to make locust legs. Repeat for the other two sets of holes. (You may want to put a dot of glue in each hole to help hold the legs in place.)

4. Help each child glue two green pompoms on top of one end of the tube. Glue two wiggly eyes in the center of the pompoms.

PRESCHOOL CONNECTION

Clean up the craft supplies. Let the locusts dry on the table while you read Exodus 7:14–12:30 from a preschool-friendly picture Bible. Then ask:

• **What would it be like to have bugs all over your house?**

• **How do you think the Egyptians felt about having locusts all over their houses and land?**

• **Why did God send the locusts to Egypt?**

Say: **Locusts make a quiet, chirping sound. You have to listen carefully to hear a locust. Pharaoh should have listened carefully to God and obeyed him. God is pleased when we listen and obey his ways.**

WOWS that work

Give each child a plastic knife and fork. Show children how to scrape the tines of the fork over the rough "cutting" edge of the knife to make the sound of a locust chirping.

MOSES PLEADS WITH PHARAOH

Exodus 7:14—12:30

What Kids Will Do: Make Moses and Pharaoh wooden spoon puppets.

What Kids Will Need: wooden spoons, wiggly eyes, pompoms, felt, yarn, sequins, metallic paper, craft glue, markers

Preparation Place: Make a sample craft ahead of time to give children an idea of what to make. Then set out all supplies on a table.

EASY Steps

MOSES AND PHARAOH SPOON PUPPETS

1. Give each child two wooden spoons.

2. Let children use markers to draw a smiling face on the back of one spoon and a frowning face on the back of the other spoon.

3. Guide children in using the assorted craft supplies to decorate the smiling spoon puppet to look like Moses and the frowning spoon puppet to look like a king—Pharaoh.

PRESCHOOL CONNECTION

Clean up the craft supplies, and let the puppets dry on the table while you read Exodus 7:14–12:30 from a preschool-friendly picture Bible. Then ask:

· **What does it mean to be stubborn?**

· **How can stubbornness get you into trouble?**

· **How do you think God felt when Pharaoh was being so stubborn?**

Say: **God told Moses to go to the Pharaoh of Egypt and tell him to free the Israelite people. Pharaoh was very stubborn—he did not want to let the people go because they were his slaves. God had to punish the Egyptians seven times before Pharaoh agreed to free God's people. God wants us to be obedient and follow his ways. When you use your puppets, you can remember to love and serve God and to not be stubborn!**

that work

Let children use the puppets to role-play the story of Moses pleading with Pharaoh. Children can hold up their Moses puppets and say, "Let my people go!" and hold up their Pharaoh puppets and say, "No!"

MOSES CROSSES THE RED SEA
Exodus 13:17–14:31

What Kids Will Do: Make paper plate chariots like the ones driven by Pharaoh's army.

What Kids Will Need: small paper plates, black construction paper, glue, two 9-inch pieces of chenille wire, crayons, child-safe scissors

Preparation Place: Set out all the supplies on a table where children can easily reach them.

EASY Steps — CHARGING CHARIOTS

1. Give each child a small paper plate. Direct children to color the backs of their plates black.

2. Help children cut their plates in half and glue the rims together.

3. Guide children as they each cut two large circles from black construction paper. Children should each glue one circle to each side of the plate rim.

4. Let children bend their two chenille wires together to make stick men to place inside their chariots.

PRESCHOOL CONNECTION

Put away the craft supplies. Open your Bible to Exodus 13:17–14:31, and show children the words. Then tell children the Bible story in your own words. Then ask:

• **How can you tell if someone is angry?**

• **What do you do when someone chases you?**

• **How did God take care of the Israelites when the angry Pharaoh was chasing them?**

Say: **Pharaoh finally said God's people could leave Egypt. Then he changed his mind, so he got in his chariot and started chasing them. When Moses reached the Red Sea, God performed a miracle! God opened up the Red Sea and let Moses and the Israelites go across. But when Pharaoh and *his* chariots got there, the water rushed back into the Red Sea and swallowed them up. God took care of his people at the Red Sea, and God takes care of his people today!**

Lead the children in a prayer, thanking God for taking care of them.

MOSES CROSSES THE RED SEA
Exodus 13:17—14:31

What Kids Will Do: Make maracas to celebrate God's miracle.

What Kids Will Need: 2 paper (or plastic) cups, dry beans, aluminum foil, stickers, tape

Preparation Place: Set all supplies on a table where children can easily reach them.

EASY Steps   PRAISE MARACAS

1. Give each child two cups. Let each child put a handful of beans in one cup. Help children tape the cups rim to rim.

2. Allow children to wrap the cups in aluminum foil.

3. Direct children to decorate the outside of the foil with stickers.

PRESCHOOL CONNECTION

Clean up the craft supplies. Open your Bible to Exodus 13:17—14:31, and show children the words. Then tell the story in your own preschool-friendly words. Then ask:

· **How do you show you are happy?**

· **When is a good time to sing praises?**

· **What are some other ways you can praise God?**

Say: **When the Israelites were safe on the other side of the Red Sea, they were happy! They knew God had taken care of them, and they wanted to show their thankfulness, so they sang praises. We can show God our love and praise by singing and making joyful noises to God!**

Lead the children in waving their arms and saying, "Praise be to God!"

Let the children pretend to be the Israelites as they use their maracas and sing this song of praise to the tune of "B-I-N-G-O."

God brought us out of
  Egypt's land
And safe across the Red Sea!
We praise and thank you,
  Lord!
We praise and thank you,
  Lord!
We praise and thank you,
  Lord!
We'll praise your name
  forever!

MOSES CROSSES THE RED SEA
Exodus 13:17–14:31

What Kids Will Do: Make a cloud and flames to remember how God appeared to the Israelites.

What Kids Will Need: large craft sticks, 6x9-inch sheets of white craft foam, cotton balls, 1-inch squares of red and yellow tissue paper, glue, paper plates, marker, child-safe scissors

Preparation Place: Trace a simple cloud shape on each sheet of craft foam. Squeeze glue onto several paper plates.

EASY Steps

PILLAR OF CLOUD, PILLAR OF FIRE

1. Let children cut the cloud shape from craft foam.

2. Allow children to glue the cloud shape to a craft stick.

3. Have children lightly crumple the tissue paper pieces and then dip the papers in the glue and glue them to the cloud shape. (Children should glue the tissue paper to the side where the stick is not showing. The "clouds" can cover up the stick on the other side.)

3. Show children how to turn over the cloud shape and glue cotton balls to the other side.

FRONT   BACK

WOWS *that work*

Let children hold up their pillars of cloud as they march around your classroom. Turn off the lights, and have them hold the pillars of fire while they lie down and pretend to sleep.

PRESCHOOL CONNECTION

Clean up the craft supplies, and set the crafts aside to dry. Open your Bible to Exodus 13:17–14:31, and show children the words. Then tell the story in your own preschool-friendly words. Then ask:

• **When you take a trip, how do you know where to go?**

• **What can you use to keep from getting lost?**

• **How does God help you know the right things to do?**

Say: **When Moses and the Israelites left Egypt, they weren't sure where to go. God put a pillar of cloud in the sky to follow during the day and a pillar of fire to follow at night. God led them to the Red Sea and away from Pharaoh and his men. God guides us by giving us the Bible and wonderful Christian teachers, parents, and friends.**

GOD GIVES MOSES THE TEN COMMANDMENTS
Exodus 19:16—20:21

What Kids Will Do: Create stained-glass cookie decorations.

What Kids Will Need: refrigerated cookie dough, colorful hard candies (such as Jolly Ranchers), baking sheets, aluminum foil, paper plates, plastic spoons, resealable plastic bags, cookie cutters, cooking spray, rolling pins, flour, oven

Preparation Place: Set out the supplies for this craft near a kitchen. Cover baking sheets with aluminum foil. Have children wash their hands before beginning this craft snack.

EASY Steps

SABBATH DAY STAINED GLASS

1. Give each child a paper plate with a little flour on it (to keep the dough from sticking) and a ball of dough. Have each child use his or her hands to roll out the dough into ropes.

2. Spray cookie cutters with the cooking spray, then let the children each choose one to work with.

3. Have the children set their cookie cutters on a foil-covered baking sheet. Be sure to leave adequate space between each cookie cutter. Then help the children to press their dough ropes *around* the greased cookie cutters. Once the dough outlines have been made, help each child carefully remove the cookie cutter.

4. Then give each child a sealed plastic bag of hard, colored candies. Help children use a rolling pin to crush the candies. Then children may scoop out the candy pieces with a spoon and place them in the dough outlines. Bake at 350 degrees for about five to six minutes, until the candy has melted.

PRESCHOOL CONNECTION

When children have finished, collect craft supplies. While the cookies cool, read Exodus 19:16–20:21 aloud from an easy-to-understand Bible translation so children know the passage is in God's Word. Then ask:

• **On what day does your family go to church?**

• **Does your family like to do other special things together on that day?**

Say: **God told Moses ten things that make him very happy. One of those ten things God said was to keep the Sabbath day holy. That means we should set aside one special day each week to remember God and rest. Many people go to church to learn more about God on the Sabbath day. Many churches are beautiful buildings with stained-glass windows in them, so you can take your stained-glass cookie home and hold it up to your window to remember that God wants us remember his special day each week.**

Let children take their cookies home rather than eat them in class. Have children use their cookies to tell their parents about God's special rules.

WOWS that work

If you don't have access to a kitchen, have children glue torn-up pieces of colored tissue paper to clear plastic lids. Simply punch a hole in the top of each lid and tie a ribbon through to hang in windows for the same colorful effect.

GOD GIVES MOSES THE TEN COMMANDMENTS
Exodus 19:16–20:21

What Kids Will Do: Create "hug and kiss" roses for their parents as a way to honor them.

What Kids Will Need: plastic spoons, Hershey's Hugs, Hershey's Kisses, red-colored plastic wrap, glue sticks, green construction paper, curling ribbon

Preparation Place: Set out all supplies where children can easily reach them.

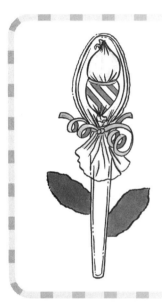

EASY Steps — LOVE IS SWEET

1. Give each child a plastic spoon. Have the children rub the glue sticks over the inside "bowls" of their spoons.

2. Demonstrate how to set one Hershey's Kiss and one Hershey's Hug inside the bowl of the spoon so that the flat parts of the candies are touching each other.

3. Give each child a small square of red plastic wrap. Help children place their spoons on the plastic wrap and wrap up the candy end. Have children hold the plastic wrap in place over the tops of their spoons.

4. As the children hold their wrapped spoons, tie a piece of curling ribbon around the neck of the spoon to hold the plastic wrap in place. Let children tear green leaves from construction paper and glue them to the "stem" of the flower.

Permission to photocopy this box from *The Encyclopedia of Bible Crafts for Preschoolers* granted for local church use.
Copyright © Group Publishing, Inc., P.O. Box 481, Loveland, CO 80539. www.grouppublishing.com

PRESCHOOL CONNECTION

When children have finished, collect craft supplies. Read Exodus 19:16–20:21 aloud from the Bible so children know the passage is in God's Word. Then ask:

• **What are some ways your parents show you that they love you?**

• **What are some ways you can show your parents that you love them?**

• **How does it make God feel when we show our parents how much we love them? What other ways can we make God feel happy?**

Say: **God told Moses ten things that make him very happy. One of those ten things God said was to honor our mommies and daddies. To honor people means we tell them thank you. We can tell our mommies and daddies thank you for loving us so very much and taking such good care of us. One way to thank our parents is to give them special gifts like hugs or kisses or even these special flowers we just made! Let's thank God for giving us our mommies and daddies or other people who take care of us. We can ask God to help us find new ways to thank them for loving us.**

Lead children in a prayer, thanking God for giving us our parents or other caregivers.

For more decorative roses, have children wrap green chenille wires around the stems of their spoons. They may also want to make several of the roses and tie them together to make a bouquet.

GOD GIVES MOSES THE TEN COMMANDMENTS

Exodus 19:16–20:21

What Kids Will Do: Create scepters to remind them of God's majesty.

What Kids Will Need: empty paper towel rolls, large pompoms, 5-inch paper stars, glitter glue, markers, curling ribbon, newspaper, scissors

Preparation Place: Cover tables with newspaper. Set all supplies where children can easily reach them.

EASY Steps SPECIAL SCEPTERS

1. Give each child an empty paper towel tube. Encourage children to color their tubes in brilliant colors. Once they have finished, write children's names on the insides of the rolls.

2. Have each child glue a paper star over one end of his or her tube. Encourage children to decorate the top of the star with glitter glue.

3. Give each child a large pompom. Let children press the pom-pom onto the top of the star, making sure the glitter glue is still wet.

4. Give each child a length of curling ribbon, and help kids tie the ribbons around their tubes near the stars. Then curl the ends of the ribbon.

PRESCHOOL CONNECTION

When children have finished, collect craft supplies. Read Exodus 19:16–20:21 aloud from the Bible so children know the passage is in God's Word. Then ask:

• **What types of people normally carry fancy scepters?**

• **How do scepters make people feel when they carry them?**

• **How do you think a king or queen would feel if everybody carried around a scepter, not just the king or queen?**

Say: **God told Moses ten things that make him very happy. One of those ten things God said was to not worship any other gods. That means God needs to be the most important thing in our lives. God is King of kings! We can show that God is number one in our lives by obeying his commandments and loving *everyone*, even when it's hard.**

Let children take turns gently touching classmates on the shoulder with their scepters. As they do, let each child say, "Remember, God is the King."

To make a more magnificent scepter, have children wrap their paper towel rolls in gold foil. Then have them place a large Styrofoam ball on top and cover the ball with glitter glue.

NUMBERS

MOSES SENDS SPIES INTO THE PROMISED LAND
Numbers 13:1–14:23

What Kids Will Do: Make magnifying spyglasses as they learn about the spies who went into the Promised Land.

What Kids Will Need: small paper plates, crayons or markers, scissors, craft sticks, cellophane, tape, glue, child-safe scissors

Preparation Place: Draw a large circle on each small paper plate, around the inside of the rim. You'll need two of these plates for each child. Set scissors in a place where children can easily share.

 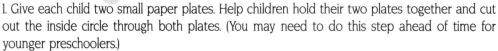 **EASY Steps — MAGNIFYING SPYGLASS**

1. Give each child two small paper plates. Help children hold their two plates together and cut out the inside circle through both plates. (You may need to do this step ahead of time for younger preschoolers.)

2. Give each child a piece of cellophane. Have children glue or tape the cellophane to one of the plate rims. Then have them attach a craft stick to the edge of the circle, on top of the cellophane.

3. Help children glue or tape together the two circles so that they are aligned, creating a magnifying glass.

4. Encourage children to use scissors to trim off the excess cellophane from around the two plates.

PRESCHOOL CONNECTION

When children have finished, collect craft supplies. Read Numbers 13:1–14:23 aloud from an easy-to-understand translation of the Bible so children know the passage is in God's Word. Then ask:

· **How do you think it would feel to be a spy?**

· **What types of things do you think Moses' spies saw in the Promised Land?**

Say: **God had a special job for the spies, and God has special jobs for each of us. God wants us to look around for people who need love.**

Let each child peer through his or her spyglass and say one way to share God's love.

MOSES SENDS SPIES INTO THE PROMISED LAND

Numbers 13:1–14:23

What Kids Will Do: Create a pair of cool spy sunglasses.

What Kids Will Need: children's sunglasses, fruit-shaped or other nature stickers, permanent marker

Preparation Place: Set out supplies where children can easily reach them.

EASY Steps — SECRET AGENT SUNGLASSES

1. Give each child a pair of child-sized sunglasses. Hand each child a strip of fruit-shaped or other nature item stickers to use in decorating their glasses.

2. Have children place their fruit stickers on the lenses of their sunglasses. Be sure to encourage them to keep the stickers around the edges of the lenses, leaving space to look through.

3. Once glasses are finished, write each child's name somewhere on his or her glasses using permanent marker.

PRESCHOOL CONNECTION

When children have finished, collect craft supplies. Read Numbers 13:1–14:23 aloud from an easy-to-understand translation of the Bible so children know the passage is in God's Word. Then ask:

- **Do you think Moses' spies wore disguises like sunglasses or wigs? Why or why not?**
- **Why were the spies so afraid?**
- **What are some things you're afraid of?**

Say: **Moses' spies saw many great things in the Promised Land, like strange new fruits and milk and honey. But they couldn't enjoy these great things because they were so afraid of the giant people they saw there. Sometimes we can't see the good things God has given us because all we can see are the scary things. Let's ask God to help us still see the good things he has given us—like our mommies and daddies, our friends, and food to eat—even when there are big scary things going on around us.**

Lead children in a prayer, asking God to help the children see the good God has made, even in bad situations.

For extra pizazz, children can attach chenille wire around the arms of the glasses, bending them into curls or other fun shapes.

MOSES SENDS SPIES INTO THE PROMISED LAND

Numbers 13:1—14:23

What Kids Will Do: Create toy spies to remind them of the Israelite spies.

What Kids Will Need: plastic garbage bags, string, hole punch, 1 rounded-head clothespin per child, ruler, pencil, scissors, fine-tipped markers

Preparation Place: Cut the garbage bags into 14x14-inch squares. Then punch one hole at each of the four corners of each square. Be sure to leave about ½-inch from the edges. Cut string into 12-inch lengths.

 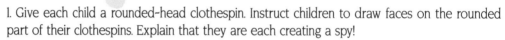

EASY Steps   FLYING SPIES

1. Give each child a rounded-head clothespin. Instruct children to draw faces on the rounded part of their clothespins. Explain that they are each creating a spy!

2. Give each child four pieces of string. Help children put one end of string through each hole and tie into a knot. Then bring the bottom ends of the strings together and tie them into a knot.

3. Have children slide their clothespin spies onto the knot. If children have made their knots too large, they may need to tie their spies onto the knots.

4. Help children fold their "parachutes" in half diagonally. Direct children to stand on a step stool. Then let each child throw his or her spy up and watch it land in a place to explore!

PRESCHOOL CONNECTION

When children have finished, collect crafts supplies. Read Numbers 13:1—14:23 aloud from an easy-to-understand translation of the Bible so children know the passage is in God's Word. Then ask:

· **How does it feel to visit someplace for the first time?**

· **What are some things you can do if you feel afraid when you visit a new place?**

Say: **Moses' spies were excited by the many great things they found when they explored the Promised Land. But they also felt afraid. God wanted the spies to be brave and trust him! Let's remember that God helps us be brave.**

Lead children in singing the following song to the tune of "Deep and Wide."

I'll trust God.

I'll trust God.

God is with me everywhere I go!

I'll trust God.

I'll trust God.

God is with me everywhere I go!

Repeat the song, this time singing "I'll be brave" instead of "I'll trust God."

BALAAM'S DONKEY TALKS
Numbers 22

What Kids Will Do: Create a donkey-face snack.

What Kids Will Need: red or yellow apples, caramel dip, large marshmallows, paring knife, baby carrots, raisins, paper plates, plastic knives, newspaper

Preparation Place: Cover table tops with newspaper or plastic tablecloths. Set out bowls of apples (cut into eighths), marshmallows, raisins, baby carrots, and caramel dip. Place plastic knives and paper plates where children can easily reach and share.

EASY Steps   HAPPY DONKEYS

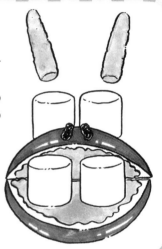

1. Give each child two slices of apple, and have kids cover one side of each slice with the caramel. Direct children to set the apples on a plate, with the plain, cut sides flat against the plate.

2. Have children set two large marshmallows in the middle of one apple slice, sticking them to the caramel. Then help children place their two slices together so that the apple skins are to the outside and the sides with caramel are touching.

3. Let children put a small dab of caramel on the skin of the top apple slice, and stick two raisin "nostrils" in place. Then have the children set two jumbo marshmallow "eyes" on the plate, just above the apple mouth. Add two baby carrots for ears, and allow children to enjoy their happy donkey snacks!

PRESCHOOL CONNECTION

When children have finished, collect craft supplies. Read Numbers 22 aloud from an easy-to-understand Bible translation, so children know the passage is in God's Word. Then ask:

• **You had to follow directions to make your snack; Balaam had to follow directions too! Why is it good to follow directions?**

• **Balaam had a donkey that talked. What do you think your pets would say if they could talk?**

• **Balaam knew that he shouldn't put a curse on the Israelites because God told him "no." Have you ever done something that you knew you weren't supposed to do? What was it and how did it make you feel?**

Say: **God made Balaam's donkey talk because God wanted Balaam to know that he wasn't supposed to hurt the Israelites. Sometimes we know we're not supposed to do something, but it takes something big for us to listen to God and do what's right. That makes God feel sad. He wants us to do what's right, right away! Let's ask God to help us to do the right thing and make choices that make God as happy as our happy face snacks!**

Lead children in a prayer, asking God to help the children make right decisions so that they can make God happy with the things they do and say.

BALAAM'S DONKEY TALKS
Numbers 22

What Kids Will Do: Create donkey puppets to remember how God let Balaam's donkey speak.

What Kids Will Need: spring clothespins, brown markers, wiggly eyes, glue, white paper, scissors, newspaper

Preparation Place: Cover tabletops with newspaper, and set out all supplies where children can easily reach them.

 **TALKING DONKEY PUPPETS**

1. Give each child a spring clothespin and a brown marker. Have the children color their clothespins.

2. Direct children to put two drops of glue just before the hinge on the top of their clothespins. Give each child two wiggly eyes to press on top of the glue. (For younger preschoolers, use small pompoms instead.)

3. Show the children how to cut out several small rectangles from the white paper, and then have the children glue them around the opening of the clothespins as "teeth."

4. Demonstrate how to make the donkey talk by squeezing its ears together, opening and closing the clothespin. For younger preschoolers, you may want to wrap masking tape thickly around each piece of the "mouth" in order to avoid finger-pinching.

PRESCHOOL CONNECTION

When children have finished, collect craft supplies. Read Numbers 22 aloud from an easy-to-understand Bible translation so children know the passage is in God's Word. Then ask:

• **Why do you think God used Balaam's donkey to get Balaam's attention?**

• **How do you think you would feel if you heard your donkey talk? How do you think Balaam might've felt?**

• **Balaam knew that he shouldn't put a curse on the Israelites because God told him "no." Have you ever done something that you knew you weren't supposed to do? What was it, and how did it make you feel?**

Say: **God made Balaam's donkey talk because God wanted Balaam to know that he wasn't supposed to hurt the Israelites. Sometimes we know we're not supposed to do something, but it takes something big for us to listen to God and do what's right. That makes God feel sad. He wants us to do what's right, right away!**

Let children use their donkey crafts to tell each other, "Do what's right, [name of child]!"

To allow children to re-enact the story of Balaam and his donkey, give each child a rounded-head clothespin. Have the children draw Balaam's face on the round part of the clothespin and then wrap the pin in a small square of felt. Have children use their two clothespins together to put on a puppet show.

66

JOSHUA

JERICHO'S WALLS COME DOWN
Joshua 6:1-27

What Kids Will Do: Create edible versions of the walls of Jericho.

What Kids Will Need: rice cakes, bowls of frosting or flavored cream cheese, graham crackers, gummy bears, paper plates, wax paper

Preparation Place: Set out sheets of wax paper for children to work on. Set out plastic knives, graham cracker squares, and bowls of frosting or flavored cream cheese where children can easily reach and share.

EASY Steps   JERICHO JUBILEE

1. Give each child a paper plate with a rice cake on it. Have children spread frosting or cream cheese all over their rice cakes and on the outer edge.

2. Show children how to place the graham cracker squares in the frosting around their rice cakes to create "walls of Jericho."

3. Give each child a handful of gummy bears, and demonstrate how to line them up around the walls on the rice cakes. Encourage the children to march their bears around the walls and then make the walls "fall down" so they can then gobble them up.

Permission to photocopy this box from *The Encyclopedia of Bible Crafts for Preschoolers* granted for local church use.
Copyright © Group Publishing, Inc., P.O. Box 481, Loveland, CO 80539. www.grouppublishing.com

PRESCHOOL CONNECTION

When children have finished, collect snack supplies. Read Joshua 6:1-27 aloud from the Bible so children know the passage is in God's Word. Then ask:

· **Have you ever walked somewhere for a very long time? Where were you?**

· **How did it feel to walk for so long? How do you think Joshua must have felt walking for seven days around the walls of Jericho?**

· **How do you think Joshua felt when the walls came crashing down?**

Say: **God told Joshua and his men to march around the walls of Jericho for six days. On the seventh day, the walls came crashing down! Joshua and his men could get into Jericho! Sometimes God wants to do special things with us, just as he did with Joshua, but it may take what seems like a very long time. But God's plans are always right and good. We can trust in God's plans.**

If you have older preschoolers, you may want to have them build up their walls of Jericho by layering mini pretzel sticks and frosting rather than simply sticking up graham cracker squares. This helps the children work on their fine motor skills.

JERICHO'S WALLS COME DOWN
Joshua 6:1–27

What Kids Will Do: Create marching shoes to remember how the Israelites marched around Jericho.

What Kids Will Need: rectangular tissue boxes, poster paint, paintbrushes, yarn, glitter glue, newspaper, paint smocks

Preparation Place: Cover table tops with newspaper. You may want to provide paint smocks for children to wear as they paint their marching shoes.

EASY Steps
JOSHUA'S MARCHING SHOES

1. Give each child two tissue boxes, and have children place their feet into the holes in the tops of their boxes. If the boxes are too big to stay on their feet, help children glue cardboard to the insides of the holes.

2. Direct children to remove the boxes from their feet. Let children paint each box with poster paint.

3. Allow the boxes to dry, and then let children decorate the outside with glitter glue. Encourage children to be creative and make imaginative designs.

4. Give each child two lengths of yarn. Tie each length into a bow for younger preschoolers, and let older preschoolers do it themselves. Then have the children glue one bow to each box as shoelaces. Have children try on their new marching shoes and carefully march around the room.

WOWS that work

If time allows, have children cut out decorations or shapes from craft foam and glue them to the outsides of their boxes. You also can punch holes in the tops of the "shoes" and let children practice lacing as well as tying.

PRESCHOOL CONNECTION

When children have finished, collect craft supplies. Read Joshua 6:1-27 aloud from the Bible so children know the passage is in God's Word. Then ask:

• **What kinds of shoes do you like to wear when you have to walk for a very long time? What kinds of shoes do you wear to church? to birthday parties? to play in snow?**

• **God is so powerful! God made the walls of Jericho fall down when the people marched around them! What are some other powerful things God has done?**

• **How do you think the people inside Jericho's walls felt when they saw their city walls come crashing down?**

Say: **God told Joshua and his men to march around the walls of Jericho for six days. Their feet were probably very, very tired! But on the seventh day, the walls came crashing down! God told Joshua to do something important, and God used his mighty power to make the hard part happen. God uses his power today to help us with hard things too. Let's thank God right now for being so powerful and mighty.**

Lead children in a prayer, thanking God for being so powerful.

JERICHO'S WALLS COME DOWN
Joshua 6:1–27

What Kids Will Do: Create musical instruments to shake as they march.

What Kids Will Need: clean, empty, clear plastic bottles (such as shampoo bottles or bottled water bottles); dry rice or beans; glue; stickers; glitter glue; curling ribbon; bowls; spoons

Preparation Place: Pour the rice or beans into bowls so children can easily use them. Set all other supplies where children can reach them.

EASY Steps   MUSICAL MARCHING MACHINES

1. Give each child a clear, clean, plastic bottle with the label removed.

2. Have the children spoon rice or beans into their bottles, filling them halfway.

3. Help each child put a small ring of glue around the inside of the bottle lid and tighten it in place. You may want to give each child a sticker to place on the outside top of the lid.

4. Once children have finished with the above steps, set out stickers and glitter glue for the children to use in decorating their bottles. Then give each child several strands of curling ribbon, and help children tie the ribbons around the necks of their bottles. Demonstrate how to shake the musical instruments and create interesting rhythms.

PRESCHOOL CONNECTION

When children have finished, collect craft supplies. Read Joshua 6:1-27 aloud from the Bible so children know the passage is in God's Word. Then ask:

• **Joshua and his men blew their trumpets as they marched around Jericho's walls. What are some other musical instruments that make loud noises?**

• **Do you think the walls would fall down if we played our new musical instruments? Why or why not?**

• **God made the walls fall down with his power! Who are some people you know who are very powerful? Did you know that God is more powerful than all of those people combined?**

Say: **God told Joshua and his men to march around the walls of Jericho for six days. On the seventh day, God told them to march around the walls seven times, blowing their trumpets. Joshua and his men did, and the walls came crashing down! God told Joshua to do something important, and God used his mighty power to make the hard part happen. I'm glad we serve a God who is so mighty!**

Lead children in shaking their instruments and singing praise songs, thanking God for his might.

GOD GIVES GIDEON VICTORY
Judges 6:1–16; 7:1–24

What Kids Will Do: Create torches as reminders of Gideon's jars with torches inside.

What Kids Will Need: empty paper towel tubes; red, yellow, and orange tissue paper; markers; stickers

Preparation Place: Set out all supplies where children can easily reach them.

 **EASY Steps** **GIDEON'S TORCHES**

1. Give each child an empty paper towel tube, and write his or her name on it. Have the children decorate their tubes with markers and stickers.

2. Let children take several sheets of each color of tissue paper and tuck them inside the paper towel rolls. Help children then fan out the tissue paper to look like flames.

3. Lead children in marching around the room with their torches, reminding them of Gideon and his men.

PRESCHOOL CONNECTION

When children have finished, collect craft supplies. Read Judges 6:1-16; 7:1-24 aloud from an easy-to-understand Bible translation so children know the passage is in God's Word. Then ask:

• **Gideon was the weakest and youngest member in his family, and God wanted to use him! What are some other ways God can use people who aren't very old or big yet?**

• **What are some things you can do for God?**

• **Gideon's men marched with trumpets and carried empty jars with torches inside because Gideon was obeying God. What are ways you can obey God?**

Say: **God helped Gideon win a battle with just a few men. They carried empty jars with torches inside, like the torches we made today. God wanted to use Gideon to lead the men, even though he was young and not very big and strong. God can use even little people to do great big things for him! God uses people your age to do things for him every day. Let's take turns saying things we can do for God, such as help our parents or tell people about God.**

Lead children in sharing ways they can serve God.

WOWS that work

For an illuminated look in the torches, use colored cellophane or plastic wrap instead of tissue paper, and then have children hold tiny flashlights inside the paper towel rolls to create the look of flames.

GOD GIVES GIDEON VICTORY

Judges 6:1–16; 7:1–24

What Kids Will Do: Create victory medallions as reminders of Gideon's victory.

What Kids Will Need: construction paper, frozen-juice can lids, scissors, glue, glitter glue, markers, ribbon, masking tape, newspaper

Preparation Place: Cover tabletops with newspaper. Set all supplies where children can easily reach them.

EASY Steps · VICTORY MEDALS

1. Give each child a frozen-juice can lid. Show the children how to trace their lids onto pieces of construction paper and then cut out the circles. (For younger children, you may want to have the circles pre-cut.)

2. Have children glue the paper circles onto the juice lids. Help children draw the letter "G" in the middle of their circles.

3. Encourage children to decorate the papers on the lids with markers and glitter glue.

4. Give each child a yard of ribbon that can fit loosely around his or her neck. Help children tape the ribbon ends to the back of the juice lids.

PRESCHOOL CONNECTION

When children have finished, collect craft supplies. Read Judges 6:1-16; 7:1-24 aloud from a preschool-friendly Bible so children know the passage is in God's Word. Then ask:

· **Have you ever received a prize or special award like a sticker for doing something? What did you do to receive it?**

· **How does it make you feel to win at something?**

· **God helped Gideon win a battle with only a very few men in his army. How do you think it made Gideon feel to win the battle?**

Say: **God gave Gideon victory in a battle that seemed impossible. Victory means that God helped him win. Sometimes people who win things get to wear special medals that show they've won. We made a special medal today with a "G" on it. God's name starts with a "G."** (Help children sound out "G—God.") **God helps all of us have victory with battles we have to face in our lives. If we're afraid of something, we can remember that Gideon was probably pretty afraid, too, but God helped Gideon, and God will help us, too. Let's do a cheer to remember that God helps us have victory when life gets hard.**

Lead children in the following cheer:

G-O-D,

God loves me!

He leads us all

To victory!

To make special winners' medals, give children three pieces of ribbon or yarn in red, white, and blue. Have the children twist them together before taping them down.

GOD GIVES GIDEON VICTORY
Judges 6:1–16; 7:1–24

What Kids Will Do: Create edible trumpets as they learn how Gideon's army frightened its enemy.

What Kids Will Need: sugar ice cream cones, cake batter, frosting, decorative candies, Skittles candies, plastic knives, paper plates, muffin tins, oven

Preparation Place: Before children arrive, mix up your favorite cake batter and pour it into sugar ice cream cones so that the cones are three-fourths filled. Set the filled cones in muffin tins, and bake according to the cake batter recipe. Set out frosting and plastic knives in a place where children can easily reach and share.

EASY Steps — TRUMPETS FOR THE TUMMY

1. Give each child a cake cone. Have the children cover the cake part of their cones with frosting.

2. Encourage children to decorate the cake part of their cones by placing candies on the frosting.

3. Let children place three dabs of frosting down the outside of the cone. Give each child three Skittles candies to stick onto the frosting dots. Explain that these are the valves of the trumpet. Encourage the children to pretend to blow their trumpets and push the "valves" before eating these yummy musical treats.

PRESCHOOL CONNECTION

When children have finished, collect snack supplies. Read Judges 6:1-16; 7:1-24 aloud from an easy-to-understand Bible translation so children know the passage is in God's Word. Then ask:

• **When Gideon's men blew their trumpets, it was a signal for God to win the battle for Gideon. What is a signal? What does a signal do?**

• **What are some signals you have seen your parents or teachers give for you to do something?**

• **What are some other times you have seen trumpets? What is your favorite musical instrument?**

Say: **God gave Gideon victory in a battle that seemed impossible. Gideon was afraid because he had very few men to fight a very big battle. But God told Gideon that when he arrived at the Midianite camp, Gideon and his men were to blow their trumpets. And they did. And God fought the battle for Gideon and won! All Gideon had to do was obey God's command. When we obey God's commands, God gives us victory too. Victory means that God helps us win. Let's all ask God to help us not be afraid of our battles and pray for God to help us obey his commands.**

Lead children in a prayer, asking God to help us not be afraid and to pray for help in obeying his commands, just as Gideon obeyed.

WOWS that work
In warm weather, a great alternative to this treat is to use Drumstick ice cream treats in place of the cake cones. Skip the step in adding frosting and decorative candies, and simply have the children add the Skittles candy valves. Be sure to have bowls handy for kids to eat their treats over.

GOD GIVES SAMSON A SPECIAL GIFT

Judges 15:9-16

What Kids Will Do: Create Samson lollipops and cut their hair.

What Kids Will Need: large, hard suckers; frosting; plastic knives; raisins or other smaller candies or dried fruit; shoestring licorice; child-safe scissors; paper plates; plastic wrap; wax paper; bowls

Preparation Place: Set a sheet of wax paper at each child's place. Set out bowls of frosting and plastic knives in a place where children can easily reach and share. Also set out the small candies or dried fruit.

EASY Steps — BARBERSHOP SAMSON

1. Give each child a large, hard lollipop.

2. Show the children how to spread frosting with a plastic knife over one side of the lollipop, not including the stick.

3. Have children create Samson's face by arranging the candies or dried fruit on the frosted side of their lollipops.

4. Once children have created their faces, give each child seven 2- to 3-inch lengths of licorice. Have children press the licorice to the frosting on the outside of the lollipop faces as Samson's seven braids of hair. Allow children to cut a few strands of licorice using child-safe scissors. Set the lollipops on paper plates, and cover them with plastic wrap.

PRESCHOOL CONNECTION

When children have finished, collect craft supplies. Read Judges 15:9-16; 16:4-30 aloud from the Bible so children know the passage is in God's Word. Then ask:

· **What special gift did God give to Samson?**

· **What are some special gifts God has given you?**

· **How would it feel to have a special gift taken away? How do you think Samson felt when his hair was cut and his gift went away?**

Say: **God gave Samson a special gift of strength. God gives each of us special gifts too. Some of can run really fast. Some of us can draw well or make amazing buildings with blocks. Some of us can share really well. I'm glad God has given you such wonderful gifts!**

These lollipops make excellent gifts, if children can resist the temptation to gobble them up after creating them! Cut a large enough square of colored cellophane to wrap around the decorated sucker. Use a decorative ribbon to tie the cellophane in place. Children may also want to create gift tags that they can attach to the lollipop sticks and then give the lollipops as special gifts to people they love.

GOD GIVES SAMSON A SPECIAL GIFT

Judges 15:9-16

What Kids Will Do: Create reminders of God's gifts by making marble-painted gift bags.

What Kids Will Need: plain-colored gift bags, marbles, liquid tempera paint, shallow containers, plastic spoons, tissue paper, large gift boxes, newspaper, marker, tissue paper, gift bows

Preparation Place: Pour a thin layer of paint into the shallow containers, and set several marbles into each container. Cover tabletops with newspaper.

EASY Steps — GOD'S GIFTS

1. Give each child a plain-colored gift bag. Set out dishes of tempera paint with several marbles in each color. Form groups of two or three children, and give each group a large gift box to use together.

2. One at a time, have children place their gift bags in the bottom of the gift box. Have each child use a spoon to take a marble from one of the dishes of paint and set it on top of the gift bag inside the box.

3. Demonstrate how to shake the gift boxes back and forth to have the painted marbles roll around on the bags. Encourage the children to repeat the process, using different-colored painted marbles to create colorful designs. Once a gift bag is decorated, set it aside to dry. Be sure to write each child's name on his or her bag.

4. Once the bags are dry, give each child several sheets of tissue paper to tuck inside his or her marbled gift bag. Then give each child a bow to place somewhere on the outside of his or her bag.

PRESCHOOL CONNECTION

When children have finished, collect craft supplies. Read Judges 15:9-16 aloud from the Bible so children know the passage is in God's Word. Then ask:

- **What was so special about Samson?**

- **What are some special things you can do?**

Say: **God gave Samson a special gift of strength. God gives us special gifts too. Whatever gifts you have, you can use them to show your love for God.** Lead children in this action rhyme:

Maybe you can skip and hop (*skip and hop in place*);

Maybe you can run (*run in place*);

Maybe you can draw so well (*pretend to draw*)

Or like to sing for fun. (*Spread arms wide.*)

Whatever it is you like to do (*shrug shoulders*)

Do it for God above. (*Point up.*)

Use your gifts to show the world (*spread arms*)

That God's the one you love. (*Hug self.*)

WOWS that work

If time allows, you may want to have children draw special pictures for their parents, showing the children using some of the gifts God has given them. Then have each child wrap up his or her picture in the tissue paper and place it inside the gift bag.

RUTH

RUTH TRUSTS GOD
Ruth 2—4

What Kids Will Do: Create wheat bouquets to remember God's provision.

What Kids Will Need: stalks of wheat, 1¾-inch miniature clay pots, florist foam or clay, ribbon, potpourri, scissors, newspaper, marker, bowls, plastic spoons

Preparation Place: Cut the florist foam so it will fit inside the clay pots. Cover table-tops with newspaper for easier cleanup. Set out supplies where children can easily reach them.

EASY Steps   BOUQUETS OF LOVE

1. Give each child a miniature clay pot, and write his or her name on the bottom.

2. Give each child a small piece of florist foam or a small ball of clay. Help children press the foam or clay into the bottoms of their pots.

3. Demonstrate how to stick the stalks of wheat individually into the foam or clay inside the pots. Each child should end up with three or four small stalks in his or her pot.

4. Once the wheat is arranged, set out small bowls of potpourri with plastic spoons in them. Help the children use the spoons to put small amounts of potpourri between the wheat stalks. Then help each child tie a small ribbon around the base of the pot.

Permission to photocopy this box from *The Encyclopedia of Bible Crafts for Preschoolers* granted for local church use.
Copyright © Group Publishing, Inc., P.O. Box 481, Loveland, CO 80539. www.grouppublishing.com

PRESCHOOL CONNECTION

When children have finished, collect crafts supplies. Read Ruth 2–4 aloud from an easy-to-understand Bible translation so children know the passage is in God's Word. Then ask:

· **How did God take care of Ruth?**

· **How does God take care of you?**

· **Ruth trusted God to give her food, a warm place to stay, and a husband to take care of her. What things do you trust God for?**

Say: **Ruth trusted God to give her wheat so that she could make bread to eat. We can trust God to give us good things to eat too. Ruth trusted God to take care of her family, and God did. We can trust God to take care of our families too. God is so good! Let's thank God for all the awesome things he gives us.**

Lead children in the following prayer, thanking God for his provision. Let each child complete this sentence: "Dear God, thank you for giving me [name something God has provided]. I love you." Close by praying, "In Jesus' name, amen."

To add a personal touch to their creations, have children use paints or glitter glue to decorate their pots. Be sure to have them paint the pots before adding the wheat, and allow the paint to dry before tying ribbons around the bases.

RUTH TRUSTS GOD
Ruth 2–4

What Kids Will Do: Create bird feeders as reminders of God's perfect provision.

What Kids Will Need: small paper plates, child-safe scissors, stapler, hole punch, yarn, birdseed, crayons or markers, newspaper, bowl

Preparation Place: Cover tables with newspaper, or have children sit on a sheet on the floor as they work on their crafts.

EASY Steps — BIRD'S CAFÉ

1. Give each child two small paper plates. Have each child fold one of the plates in half and then cut it in half on the crease.

2. Staple the half-plate onto the bottom of the whole plate, creating a pocket. Have children use crayons or markers to decorate their plates.

3. Punch two holes at the top of the whole plate, and have each child slip a piece of yarn through both holes, knotting each end to create a hanger for the "pocket."

4. Once the bird feeders are complete, set out a large bowl of birdseed, and have the children scoop some into their feeders. Demonstrate how children can hang their bird feeders outside their homes to care for God's feathered creatures.

WOWS that work

If you have a longer amount of time, try this variation. Fill muffin tins with water. Have children sprinkle raisins, berries, seeds, and nuts into the water–filled tins and then place a folded chenille–wire hanger into each cup. Freeze the muffin tins. Once they are frozen, pop out the bird–friendly treats and hang them outside. As the water melts, birds will enjoy the frozen goodies inside!

PRESCHOOL CONNECTION

When children have finished, collect craft supplies. Read Ruth 2–4 aloud from an easy-to-understand Bible translation or picture Bible so children know the passage is in God's Word. Then ask:

· **How did God care for Ruth?**

· **How can we care for God's creations?**

· **Ruth trusted God to take care of her. What are some things that you can trust God for?**

Say: **Ruth knew that she could trust God to take care of her. And God did! He gave her food to eat, a warm place to stay, and a husband who loved her; and he even took care of her family, too.**

Let children take turns each telling one way God takes care of them.

1 SAMUEL

SAMUEL LISTENS TO GOD

1 Samuel 3:1–21

What Kids Will Do: Create beds in which Samuel can sleep.

What Kids Will Need: small boxes with lids (such as jewelry boxes), fabric paint, glue, felt, scissors, cotton balls

Preparation Place: Set out all supplies where children can easily reach them.

EASY Steps   NEWS AT NIGHT

1. Give each child a small box with a lid. Show children how to take the lids off their boxes and flip the boxes upside down. Help each child put the lid on one edge of the box as if a headboard for a small bed.

2. Give each child a small piece of felt. Help each child cut the felt into a small rectangle that will fit on top of his or her box, like a blanket.

3. Encourage children to decorate the felt "blankets" with fabric paints. Allow the blankets to dry before gluing them in place on the boxes.

4. Give each child a cotton ball or a rolled-up strip of white felt. Have children glue the cotton ball or felt to the box, touching the headboard, to create a pillow for the bed.

PRESCHOOL CONNECTION

When children have finished, collect craft supplies. Read 1 Samuel 3:1-21 aloud from the Bible so children know the passage is in God's Word. Then ask:

• **Samuel heard God's voice at night when he was in bed. What are some noises you hear when you are in bed?**

• **How would you feel if God talked to you? What would you do?**

• **When do you like to talk to God?**

Say: **Samuel heard God's voice when he was lying in bed one night. God had an important message for Samuel. God has important messages for us, too. Everything God wants to say to us is right there in our Bible. God wants us to hear and obey the things he tells us in the Bible.**

Let children take turns handing the Bible to each other. Each time the Bible is passed, lead children in saying, "Listen and obey."

WOWS that work

To create a personal puppet show for the children, help each child poke a hole through the box part of the bed before covering it with the felt blanket. Once the bed is assembled, you may use a pen to draw a face on each child's finger. Children can poke their fingers through the box and re-enact the Bible story of Samuel waking up to listen to God.

SAMUEL LISTENS TO GOD
1 Samuel 3:1-21

What Kids Will Do: Create listening ears to help them remember to listen to God.

What Kids Will Need: child-sized headbands; tape; small paper plates; child-safe scissors; stickers of things that make noise (such as birds, musical notes, or children); crayons

Preparation Place: Set out all supplies where children can easily reach them.

EASY Steps — SAMUEL'S LISTENING EARS

1. Give each child a headband and a small paper plate.

2. Help children fold their paper plates in half and cut along the fold to make two half-circles.

3. Encourage children to color each half-circle to make ears. Let children be creative in the colors they choose. Distribute stickers, and have children place the stickers on their plates.

4. Help the children tape the "ears" to the outside of both sides of the headband, close to the bottom. The paper plates should line up on the headband to be ears when the preschooler puts the headband on his or her head.

PRESCHOOL CONNECTION

When children have finished, collect craft supplies. Read 1 Samuel 3:1-21 aloud from an easy-to-understand Bible translation so children know the passage is in God's Word. Then ask:

· **What are some things you like to listen to?**

· **What are some things you don't enjoy hearing?**

· **How do you think it would feel to hear God's voice? What do you think his voice would sound like?**

Say: **Samuel heard God's voice when he was lying in bed one night. Samuel thought Eli was calling him! But Eli knew that God had an important message for Samuel and told Samuel to put on his listening ears so he could hear what God had to say. Let's listen to God and do the things God wants us to do.**

Have children wear their Listening Ears as you lead them in the following song, to the tune of "Frère Jacques."

I am listening.

I am listening

To the Lord,

To the Lord.

I want to obey God.

I want to obey God

Every day,

Every day.

DAVID BECOMES KING

1 Samuel 16:1–16

What Kids Will Do: Create crowns fit for a king.

What Kids Will Need: bendable party garland, colorful foam shapes, hole punch, scissors

Preparation Place: Cut 1 foot of bendable party garland for each child. Use a hole punch to make a hole in the center of each foam shape. You'll need about ten shapes per child.

EASY Steps — KINGLY CROWNS

1. Give each child a length of garland and ten foam shapes.

2. Show children how to string the shapes onto their garland and position the shapes evenly.

3. Help children tightly twist the ends of their garland together and then place the crowns on their heads. (You can adjust the size of the crown simply by twisting the garland.)

PRESCHOOL CONNECTION

Have children help you clean up the craft supplies. Gather children in a circle, wearing their crowns. Read 1 Samuel 16:1-16 from an easy-to-understand Bible translation.

Say: **God knew that he wanted David to be a king, even when David was just a boy. God sent a man named Samuel to teach David about God's plans. God had special plans for David.** Ask:

• **What special plans do you think God might have for you?**

• **Samuel helped David learn about God. Who helps you learn about God?**

• **David was special to God, even when he was just a boy. How do you know you're special to God?**

Say: **David was special to God, and so are you! God had plans for David, and he has plans for you! Let's thank God for loving us so much.**

Lead children in the following rhyme to thank God.

God, you love us.

Yes, it's true!

You know all that we can do.

Thank you for your plans so good.

We'll obey you like we should.

In Jesus' name, amen.

DAVID BECOMES KING
1 Samuel 16:1-16

What Kids Will Do: Make pictures that show they're special to God.

What Kids Will Need: construction paper, scissors, glue sticks, fine-tipped washable markers, crayons

Preparation Place: Cut out people shapes from construction paper. Cut out hearts from red construction paper. Set all supplies on a table where children can easily reach them.

EASY Steps

SPECIAL TO GOD

1. Give each child a paper person. Write the child's name on the back of his or her person.

2. Encourage children to decorate the paper people to look like themselves.

3. Show children how to glue the top edge of a paper heart to the top of the paper person's head so the heart can be lifted up like a flap.

Permission to photocopy this box from *The Encyclopedia of Bible Crafts for Preschoolers* granted for local church use.
Copyright © Group Publishing, Inc., P.O. Box 481, Loveland, CO 80539. www.grouppublishing.com

Instead of construction paper hearts, give each child a heart cut from wax paper. Let children tape the hearts over their people shapes to show that God looks into our hearts to see what we're like.

PRESCHOOL CONNECTION

Collect the craft supplies when children have finished.

Say: **When David was just a boy, God had already chosen him to be king when he got a little older. God sent a man named Samuel to let David know he had been chosen. When Samuel got to David's house, the family thought he would choose one of David's older brothers. Listen to what the Bible tells us that God said about one of David's brothers.**

Read 1 Samuel 16:1-16 aloud from the Bible. Then ask:

• **According to this verse, what does God look at when he looks at people?**

• **What does it mean to look at someone's heart?**

• **How can we look at others' hearts too?**

Say: **God cares about what's inside a person, not about how people look! We can try to care about people the same way, by caring about what's inside instead of how they look. Take your paper people home with you to remind you that God looks at the heart.**

DAVID BECOMES KING
1 Samuel 16:1–16

What Kids Will Do: Create "dial-a-pictures" to show how many brothers David had.

What Kids Will Need: paper plates, paper fasteners, scissors, circle stickers, small heart stickers, fine-tipped markers

Preparation Place: For each child, poke a hole in the center of two paper plates. On one of the plates, cut a 3-inch window between the center hole and outer edge.

EASY Steps

DIAL-A-DAVID

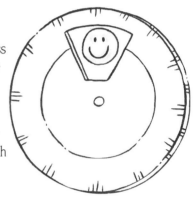

1. Show children how to place eight circle stickers equidistantly around the windowless plate, about an inch from the edge so the stickers will show through the window you've cut in the other plate.

2. Let kids decorate the circle stickers to look like the faces of David's brothers.

3. Have each child place a small heart sticker next to one circle sticker to represent David.

4. Place the "window plate" over the sticker plate, and help each child secure the two with the paper fastener. Let children turn their top plates until they see their David stickers.

PRESCHOOL CONNECTION

Have children help you clean up the craft supplies. Gather children in a circle with their crafts. Read aloud 1 Samuel 16:1-16 from a preschool-friendly Bible translation. Explain that as you mention each of Jesse's sons, children can dial their plates past a circle face. When the Bible mentions David, they can dial to the face with the heart sticker. Then ask:

• **Why did God choose David instead of his brothers?**

• **Why do you think that what's in our hearts is more important to God than how we look on the outside?**

• **Who gave each of us our special "inside" qualities?**

Say: **God made each one of us special. God cares more about what's in our hearts and how we act than he does about how we look. Let's thank God for making us special!**

Lead children in a prayer, thanking God for making each child special.

Make this craft more colorful by using colored paper plates when you cut out the windows.

DAVID DEFEATS GOLIATH
1 Samuel 17:1–50

What Kids Will Do: Create David and Goliath games.

What Kids Will Need: foam cups, 10-inch lengths of string, tape, cotton balls, poster board, scissors, crayons, markers

Preparation Place: Cut poster board into a 4-inch oval for each child. Set all supplies on a table where children can easily reach them.

EASY Steps   GOLIATH GAME

1. Give each child a cup, and let him or her poke a hole in the bottom of it. Help children thread a 10-inch length of string through the hole and tape the end to the outside bottom of the cup.

2. Help children tape a cotton ball to the opposite end of the string.

3. Let children decorate the poster board ovals to look like Goliath's face. Then tape the ovals to the outside upper edges of the cups.

4. Show children how to try to hit the Goliath face with the cotton ball, just as David hit Goliath with a stone.

WOWS
that work

Use large jingle bells instead of cotton balls to make this craft more "musically" memorable. (Just be sure the jingle bells are large enough not to pose a choking hazard.)

PRESCHOOL CONNECTION

Gather children in a circle with their crafts. Explain that the Bible tells about a time David faced a giant enemy named Goliath. Read aloud 1 Samuel 17:1-50. Ask:

· **How did David win the battle with the giant Goliath?**

· **Why do you think David was so sure he would be able to beat Goliath?**

· **Who helped David win the fight with Goliath?**

Say: **David knew that he could beat Goliath because David knew that God would help him. Just as God helped David with the big problem of facing a giant, God will help us with our problems, too. Let's talk to God about our problems right now.**

Let children pray silently about any problems they may be facing. Then encourage them to use their Goliath games at home to tell family members and friends about how God helped David.

DAVID DEFEATS GOLIATH

1 Samuel 17:1–50

What Kids Will Do: Create armor, just like David tried to wear.

What Kids Will Need: brown paper grocery bags, aluminum foil, glue sticks or tape, marker, scissors

Preparation Place: Open each bag, and cut a slit up the middle of the front. Cut a hole in the bottom for a child to put his or her head through. Then cut an armhole on each side of the bag.

EASY Steps EASY ARMOR

1. Set out sheets of aluminum foil, and let children tear or cut the foil into strips.

2. Give each child a bag, and write his or her name on it. Let children glue or tape the foil pieces to their paper bags to make suits of armor.

3. Help children put on their armor. Guide children's arms through the holes as they put on their armor like a vest.

PRESCHOOL CONNECTION

When children have finished, collect craft supplies. Read 1 Samuel 17:1-50 aloud from an easy-to-understand Bible translation so children know the passage is in God's Word. Explain that the giant Goliath was wearing heavy armor when David faced him in battle. Then ask:

• **Since Goliath was wearing all that armor, how do you think David was able to win the battle?**

• **Do you think David could have beaten Goliath without God's help? Why or why not?**

• **When is a time God has helped you face a big problem?**

Say: **Even though Goliath was wearing a lot of armor and had a sword and shield and everything, David still won the battle! David won because God helped him. God wants to help us, too! Let's thank God for being so powerful and for always being ready to help us.**

Lead children in the following rhyming prayer:

God, you are mighty. (*Flex right arm.*)

God, you are strong. (*Flex left arm.*)

I know that you'll help me (*point to self*)

All day long. (*Stretch arms wide.*)

In Jesus' name, amen.

Set out pieces of Mylar (found in the party section of most craft stores) or old Mylar balloons. Let children cut these colorful, shiny pieces to add to their armor.

DAVID DEFEATS GOLIATH
1 Samuel 17:1–50

What Kids Will Do: Create helmets as they learn that mighty Goliath wore armor and a helmet.

What Kids Will Need: large sheets of poster board, scissors, tape, stickers, crayons, washable markers

Preparation Place: Cut a poster board rectangle for each child, wide enough to fit around a child's head. In the center of each rectangle, cut two eyeholes, a nose hole, and a mouth hole.

EASY Steps — HEFTY HELMETS

1. Give each child a poster board rectangle. Write his or her name on it.

2. Let children use crayons, markers, and stickers to decorate their rectangles.

3. Fit each child's rectangle around his or her head, cutting off excess poster board in the back and loosely taping the ends together. Make sure children can see and breathe easily with their helmets on.

Permission to photocopy this box from *The Encyclopedia of Bible Crafts for Preschoolers* granted for local church use.
Copyright © Group Publishing, Inc., P.O. Box 481, Loveland, CO 80539. www.grouppublishing.com

WOWS that work

Glue Velcro fasteners to the backs of the helmets to make them easier to put on and take off.

PRESCHOOL CONNECTION

When children have finished, collect craft supplies. Have children sit in a circle, wearing their helmets. Read 1 Samuel 17:4-7 from the Bible. Then ask:

• **How do you think David felt when he saw that giant wearing a helmet and a suit of armor and carrying a big sword?**

• **Sometimes we all face scary situations. When is a time you were scared?**

• **How did God help you in that situation?**

Say: **David was able to beat Goliath because God helped David. Listen to what David said to Goliath.** Read aloud 1 Samuel 17:47-49. **David knew that God would help him, and we can know that God will help us, too! Let's thank God for always being there to help us.**

Go around the circle, and let each child take off his or her helmet and tell God, "Thank you for helping us."

DAVID AND JONATHAN ARE FRIENDS

1 Samuel 18:1–4; 19:1–7; 20:1–42

What Kids Will Do: Create mitten-puppet reminders of David and Jonathan's friendship.

What Kids Will Need: light-colored bath mittens (available at most discount stores), Velcro fasteners, paint smocks or oversized T-shirts, fabric markers, tacky craft glue, newspaper

Preparation Place: Cover a table with newspaper. Then set out the supplies where children can easily reach them.

EASY Steps   FRIENDSHIP PUPPETS

1. Distribute paint smocks or oversized T-shirts, and help children put them on. Give each child a pair of bath mittens, and explain that one mitten hand can be David and one can be his friend Jonathan.

2. Encourage children to use fabric markers to decorate the mittens, drawing facial features, hair, and so on.

3. Help children glue a Velcro fastener to the center back of each mitten, making sure to use a pair of fasteners so they stick together.

4. When the glue dries, let children put on their mitten puppets. Demonstrate how the mitten friends can stick together.

PRESCHOOL CONNECTION

Collect the craft supplies, and have children sit in a circle wearing their mitten puppets. Explain that the Bible tells us about two very good friends. Read aloud 1 Samuel 18:1-4. Then ask:

• **How can you tell that David was Jonathan's good friend? How does the Bible say Jonathan felt about David?**

• **Who is a good friend of yours? What makes that person your good friend?**

• **How do good friends treat each other?**

Say: **Jonathan and David were good friends. The Bible goes on to tell us how Jonathan helped David. Good friends help each other. Let's tell some ways we can help our friends.**

Let each child share one way he or she can help a friend.

WOWS *that work*
If you can't find bath mittens, simple knit mittens or oven mitts will work just as well.

DAVID AND JONATHAN ARE FRIENDS
1 Samuel 18:1–4; 19:1–7; 20:1–42

What Kids Will Do: Lace paper friends together to show that Jonathan and David enjoyed being together.

What Kids Will Need: light-colored poster board, scissors, hole punch, 20-inch shoelaces, marker

Preparation Place: For each child, cut two 6-inch gingerbread person shapes from light-colored poster board. Align the shapes, and punch several holes through both, at ¼-inch intervals, around the edges.

EASY Steps   LACING FRIENDS

1. Give each child a pair of poster-board people. Be sure to write the child's name on both people.

2. Let children decorate one side of one shape as David and one side of the other shape as Jonathan.

3. Demonstrate how to place the two shapes together with the decorated sides facing out. Guide children in lacing the figures together with a shoelace.

Ask a carpenter in your church to cut the gingerbread shapes out of thin wood. Let the children sand the wood smooth and then glue the shapes together.

PRESCHOOL CONNECTION

Let children practice lacing their poster-board friends together as you tell them how David and Jonathan were good friends. Read aloud 1 Samuel 18:1-4, 19:1-7; and 20:1-42 from a preschool-friendly Bible translation. Then ask:

- **How did Jonathan help his friend David?**
- **When is a time you helped a friend?**
- **Why do you think God gave us good friends?**

Say: **God gave us good friends because he loves us. Good friends help each other, just as Jonathan helped David. Let's pray to God and ask him to teach us to be good friends to each other.**

Close in prayer, asking God for help and guidance in being good friends.

DAVID AND JONATHAN ARE FRIENDS
1 Samuel 18:1–4; 19:1–7; 20:1–42

What Kids Will Do: Create quivers and arrows to remember how Jonathan sent a special message to David.

What Kids Will Need: drinking straws, 6-inch lengths of curling ribbon, scissors, tape, construction paper

Preparation Place: Set out all supplies on a table where children can easily reach them.

EASY Steps

FRIENDSHIP ARROWS

1. Give each child several drinking straws and three or four lengths of curling ribbon per straw. Go to each child, and use scissors to curl the ribbon.

2. Help children tape three or four lengths of curled ribbon to the end of each straw to make arrows.

3. Give each child a half sheet of construction paper, and demonstrate how to fold the paper in half and tape it to form a quiver. Leave one edge open.

4. Let children place their straw arrows in their paper quivers, and explain that Jonathan used a quiver of arrows to help his friend David.

PRESCHOOL CONNECTION

When children have finished, collect the craft supplies. Read aloud 1 Samuel 18:1-4, then read or paraphrase 1 Samuel 19:1-7; and 20:1-42. Then ask:

· **How did Jonathan use arrows to help his friend David?**

· **Why do friends help each other?**

· **How do you think you could help a friend this week?**

Say: **Jonathan helped David because they were good friends, and good friends help each other. God gives us good friends to help us.**

Cut the quivers out of brown material instead of construction paper, then tape or glue two edges together. Let children take turns throwing their arrows and acting out the Bible story.

1 KINGS

SOLOMON ASKS FOR WISDOM
1 Kings 2:1-4; 3:3-28

What Kids Will Do: Create footprints to remind them to follow God's ways as they grow.

What Kids Will Need: aluminum pie plates, self-hardening clay, permanent marker, newspaper, damp and dry towels

Preparation Place: Cover a section of the floor with newspaper or a sheet. Have both damp and dry towels on hand for cleanup.

EASY Steps

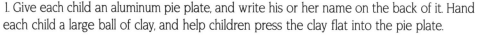

WALK-IN-THE-WAY FOOTPRINTS

1. Give each child an aluminum pie plate, and write his or her name on the back of it. Hand each child a large ball of clay, and help children press the clay flat into the pie plate.

2. Let each child remove one shoe and sock. Help each child gently place one bare foot in the clay and step down with enough pressure to make a footprint.

3. Have children wash off and dry their feet and replace their shoes and socks.

You may want to print out copies of the rhyming prayer and let children tape them to the backs of the aluminum pie plates.

PRESCHOOL CONNECTION

Tell children that the Bible tells about a very wise and smart man who wanted to walk in the ways of the Lord. Read aloud 1 Kings 2:1-4; 3:3-28 from an easy-to-understand Bible translation. Then ask:

• **Why do you think Solomon asked God for wisdom?**

• **Solomon was smart enough to know he needed God's help to make decisions. When do you need God's help?**

Say: **God will give us wisdom so we can walk in his way, just as Solomon did. Let's ask God for wisdom right now.**

Lead children in the following rhyming prayer, asking God for wisdom.

God, please give me wisdom

So I can walk in your way.

I want to do what pleases you

Every single day.

In Jesus' name, amen.

SOLOMON ASKS FOR WISDOM
1 Kings 2:1-4; 3:3-28

What Kids Will Do: Make people with "bobbin' heads" that remind them to make good choices.

What Kids Will Need: construction paper, crayons, glue, scissors

Preparation Place: Cut construction paper into 3-inch circles and 1x4-inch strips.

EASY Steps BOBBIN' HEAD PICTURES

1. Give each child a 3-inch circle of construction paper, and let him or her draw a happy face on it.

2. Distribute strips of paper, and help children accordion-fold the paper.

3. Show children how to glue one end of the paper to the back of the happy-face circle.

4. Have kids glue the other end of the paper strip to a sheet of paper. Then let children draw a body underneath the "bobbin' head" face.

PRESCHOOL CONNECTION

When children have finished, collect craft supplies. Open your Bible to 1 Kings 2:1-4; 3:3-28, and show children the words so children know the passage is in God's Word. Then tell children the story of Solomon in your own preschool-friendly words. Then ask:

· **Why do you think Solomon asked God to help him know right from wrong?**

· **When do you need help knowing right from wrong?**

· **Who can you ask for help when you don't know right from wrong?**

Say: **Solomon needed help to know right from wrong, so he asked God to help him. God knows everything and is always ready to help us know right from wrong. When you do something right, your parents might nod "yes."** Use one of the crafts to show the head nodding yes. **But when you do something wrong, your parents might shake their heads "no."** Use the craft to show the head shaking from side to side. **God wants us to make good choices.**

ELIJAH HELPS A WIDOW
1 Kings 17:7-24

What Kids Will Do: Create loaves of bread to give away.

What Kids Will Need: small paper plates, shredded wheat, softened cream cheese, spoons, self-adhesive gift tags, pens, plastic wrap

Preparation Place: Set all supplies on a clean table, where children can easily reach them. You may want to spread out a sheet and let children work on the sheet for easier cleanup.

EASY Steps   LITTLE LOAVES

1. Have children wash their hands before giving them each a small paper plate and gift tag. Help children sign their names on the tags.

2. Crumble several shredded wheat biscuits onto each child's plate, then add a spoonful of softened cream cheese.

3. Show children how to knead the ingredients together to form a dough, then demonstrate how to shape the dough into a little loaf.

4. Wrap each child's gift loaf in plastic wrap and add the gift tag. Then let children make little loaves to eat in class before they wash their hands again.

PRESCHOOL CONNECTION

Set aside the gift loaves. Then, as children enjoy the loaves they made for themselves, read aloud 1 Kings 17:7-24 from an easy-to-understand translation of the Bible. Then ask:

· **How do you think the woman felt when Elijah asked her to use the last of her flour to make him some bread?**

· **Elijah knew that God would help the woman. When has God helped you or your family?**

· **Elijah told the woman that she could trust God. Who is one person you can tell about God this week?**

Say: **Elijah helped the woman by telling her to trust God. Elijah knew that God would help her. God always comes through for us, just as he did for the woman in our Bible story. God is always ready to help us.**

ELIJAH HELPS A WIDOW
1 Kings 17:7–24

What Kids Will Do: Create prayer pockets as they learn how God provided for Elijah, the widow, and her son.

What Kids Will Need: sheets of fine sandpaper, crayons, scissors, stapler, marker

Preparation Place: Trace a slice of bread onto the back of a sheet of fine sandpaper, and cut out the pattern. Cut two patterns for each child. (Older preschoolers may be able to do this step.)

EASY Steps — PRAYER POCKETS

1. Give each child two sandpaper patterns. Write the child's name on the rough side of one pattern.

2. Show children how to place the patterns together, rough sides out. Staple the patterns together, leaving the top open to form a pocket.

3. Let children use crayons to color and decorate their pockets.

PRESCHOOL CONNECTION

Collect the craft supplies and put them away. Read aloud 1 Kings 17:7-24. Ask:

· **How did God answer Elijah's prayer in the Bible story?**

· **When has God answered your prayers?**

· **Why do you think God answers our prayers?**

Say: **God answers our prayers because he loves us. No matter how big our problems may seem, we can always talk to God. Sometimes things in our lives might be tough to go through, just as the sandpaper of our prayer pockets feels rough. But God cares about us and will always answer our prayers. Let's talk to God right now!**

Lead children in a prayer, thanking God for always listening to us and answering our prayers. Encourage children to take home their prayer pockets. Tell them to ask their parents to write prayer requests to God and put them in the pockets. Then next week they can take out the papers and see how God is answering their prayers.

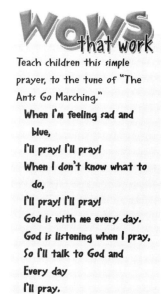

WOWS that work

Teach children this simple prayer, to the tune of "The Ants Go Marching."

When I'm feeling sad and blue,

I'll pray! I'll pray!

When I don't know what to do,

I'll pray! I'll pray!

God is with me every day.

God is listening when I pray,

So I'll talk to God and

Every day

I'll pray.

ELIJAH HELPS A WIDOW
1 Kings 17:7–24

What Kids Will Do: Make smiley bread faces to help remember that God provided food for Elijah, the widow, and her son.

What Kids Will Need: small paper plates, English muffin halves, softened flavored cream cheese, spoon, plastic knives, raisins, napkins, plastic wrap, self-adhesive gift tags, pens

Preparation Place: Set out all supplies on a clean table where children can reach them.

EASY Steps — SMILEY FACES

1. After children wash their hands, give each child an English muffin half on a small paper plate. Spoon softened flavored cream cheese onto each child's muffin half.

2. Give each child a plastic knife, and let children spread the cream cheese evenly over their muffins.

3. Let children use raisins to make smiley faces on the cream cheese, then cover each creation with plastic wrap. Attach gift tags that children have signed.

4. Let children make another smiley face muffin to eat in class.

WOWS that work

Let children decorate their smiley faces with small candies, colored mini-marshmallows, and string licorice, in addition to raisins.

PRESCHOOL CONNECTION

As children enjoy their treats, read aloud 1 Kings 17:7-24 from an easy-to-understand Bible.

Say: **In our Bible story, the woman made Elijah some bread, even though she didn't think she would have enough flour and oil to make the bread. But Elijah knew that God would help the woman, and God did! That made the woman very happy, just like our smiley treats look happy.** Ask:

• **How did God help the woman in the Bible story?**

• **How do you feel when God helps you?**

• **Why does God help us?**

Say: **God helps us because he loves us. And God's love can make us happy, just as it made the woman in the Bible story happy. Let's tell God how happy he makes us!**

Lead children in a simple cheer for God. Then pray, thanking God for loving and helping us.

ELIJAH CHALLENGES THE PROPHETS OF BAAL

1 Kings 18:16–39

What Kids Will Do: Create edible altars as they learn how God lighted Elijah's altar.

What Kids Will Need: small paper plates, wax paper, marshmallows, frosting, plastic knives, small pretzel sticks, napkins, plastic wrap, self-adhesive gift tags, pens

Preparation Place: Set out sheets of wax paper on a table for children to work on.

EASY Steps — EDIBLE ALTARS

1. Give each child a plastic knife; twelve marshmallows; and two small paper plates, one with a spoonful of frosting on it.

2. Show children how to build an altar by stacking the marshmallows in a circle, using the frosting as glue.

3. Let children spread a little frosting on the top of their altars. Then show them how to lay pretzel sticks across the tops of the altars like firewood.

4. Wrap children's creations in plastic wrap, and attach signed, self-adhesive gift tags. Then let children each make another snack to eat in class.

Permission to photocopy this box from *The Encyclopedia of Bible Crafts for Preschoolers* granted for local church use.
Copyright © Group Publishing, Inc, P.O. Box 481, Loveland, CO 80539. www.grouppublishing.com

PRESCHOOL CONNECTION

When children have finished, collect craft supplies. Let children enjoy their snacks as you read or paraphrase 1 Kings 18:16-39. Show children the passage in the Bible so they know the story comes from God's Word. Then ask:

- **How did Elijah know that God would win the challenge with the prophets of Baal?**

- **Elijah trusted God to help him. When have you trusted God to help you?**

- **How do you think God feels when we trust him?**

Say: **We can always trust God, just as Elijah did. God will never let us down. God is glad when we trust him.**

Encourage children to take their snacks home and use them to retell the story of Elijah and the prophets of Baal to their families.

WOWS that work

Let children lay a few yellow and red sugared gummy worms on top of the pretzels to look like fire.

ELIJAH CHALLENGES THE PROPHETS OF BAAL

1 Kings 18:16–39

What Kids Will Do: Create pop-up altars to remind them that Elijah's altar burst into flames.

What Kids Will Need: foam cups, markers, craft sticks, tape, yellow and red tissue paper

Preparation Place: Set out all supplies on a table where children can easily reach them.

EASY Steps   POP-UP ALTARS

1. Let each child use markers to decorate the outside of a foam cup to look like stones or bricks.

2. Help each child poke a craft stick through the bottom of the cup.

3. Direct children to tear red and yellow tissue paper into 3-inch pieces and then tape several of the pieces to the end of the craft stick inside the cup.

4. Let children pull the tissue paper "flames" inside the cup. Demonstrate how to push up the stick so the flames show and then pull it down to make the flames disappear.

PRESCHOOL CONNECTION

When children have finished, collect the craft supplies. Gather children in a circle with their crafts. Read aloud 1 Kings 18:16–39. Encourage children to use their crafts as you tell the Bible story. They can pull the flames inside the cup when you mention the prophets of Baal, and they can push the flames up when God answers Elijah's prayer. After the story, ask:

- **How did God help Elijah in this Bible story?**
- **When are times you need God's help?**
- **Elijah prayed to God for help. What can you do the next time you need God's help?**

Say: **We all need help sometimes, and God is the very best place to go for help. God is always ready to help, and he always knows just what to do. Just as God helped Elijah, God will help us! I think it's time to thank God for his help!**

Go around the circle, and let children take turns pushing up the flames in their cups as they say, "Thank you, God, for helping us."

WOWS that work

For a more realistic-looking altar, cut adhesive shelf paper that has a brick or stone pattern on it into rectangles, and attach the paper to the cups.

ELIJAH CHALLENGES THE PROPHETS OF BAAL

1 Kings 18:16-39

What Kids Will Do: Create surprise cards with "jumping flames."

What Kids Will Need: construction paper, red and yellow tissue paper, tape, crayons, markers

Preparation Place: Set out all supplies on a table where children can easily reach them.

EASY Steps

SURPRISE CARDS

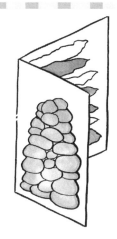

1. Help each child fold a sheet of construction paper in half to form a card.

2. Let children use crayons and markers to decorate the outsides of their cards to look like the stones of an altar.

3. Show children how to tape several pieces of crumpled red and orange tissue paper inside the cards along the fold. Make sure children write their names on their cards.

4. Show children that when they open their cards, orange and yellow flames jump up, just as flames jumped up from the altar Elijah made.

PRESCHOOL CONNECTION

Collect the craft supplies, and set them out of sight. Gather children in a circle with their cards. Read aloud 1 Kings 18:16-39. During the story, encourage children to open their cards when God sends fire to Elijah's altar. After the Bible story, ask:

· **What do you think the people thought when they saw the flames on Elijah's altar?**

· **God helped Elijah that day, and as a result, many people believed in God. How can you help other people believe in God?**

· **Who can you tell about God this week?**

Say: **Elijah trusted God to help him, and God did! Lots of people who saw what happened that day came to believe in God. When we trust God, we can show other people that it's good to believe in God.**

Form two groups, then lead children in the following cheer. Have one group stand up and do the cheer to the other group. Then let the other group stand up and do the cheer.

We believe in God—

Yes, we do!

We believe in God—

How about you?

Use red and yellow cellophane instead of tissue paper for a more "crackling" fire.

ELISHA HELPS A WIDOW AND HER SONS
2 Kings 4:1–7

What Kids Will Do: Create bottles that are never empty as they learn how God helped the widow.

What Kids Will Need: clean 12-ounce plastic bottles with caps, permanent marker, craft glue, large bowl of cooking oil, funnels, ¼-cup measuring cups, paint markers, paper towels

Preparation Place: Set all supplies where children can easily reach them.

EASY Steps   MORE-THAN-ENOUGH BOTTLES

1. Give each child a bottle and cap. Use a permanent marker to write the child's name on the bottom of his or her bottle.

2. Help children dip ¼-cup measuring cups into the bowl of cooking oil and then use funnels to pour the oil into their bottles. Keep paper towels on hand in case of spills.

3. Let children glue on the bottle caps, sealing the bottles shut.

4. Have children use paint markers to decorate their bottles.

WOWS *that work*
Set out glitter, and let each child add a pinch of glitter to the oil in the bottle.

PRESCHOOL CONNECTION

When children have finished painting, set bottles aside to dry. Open your Bible to 2 Kings 4:1-7, and tell the children the story in your own words. Then ask:

• **How can you know that there's oil in your bottles?**

• **What could your mom or dad do with this little bit of oil?**

• **Why does God give his children more than enough?**

Say: **In our Bible story, God gave the woman enough oil so she could earn money to pay her bills. That meant that her sons wouldn't have to be slaves! God took care of her needs. Then God gave her more than enough! God will take care of our needs, too. He will give us more than enough.**

ELISHA HELPS A WIDOW AND HER SONS

2 Kings 4:1-7

What Kids Will Do: Make overflowing snack cups to remember that God gave the widow more than enough oil.

What Kids Will Need: clear plastic cups (any size), marker, craft glue, tissue paper, scissors, cotton swabs, small paper plates, large plastic bowl, small crackers

Preparation Place: Cut tissue paper into 1- to 2-inch squares. Pour the craft glue onto several paper plates. Set out all supplies (except the crackers) so children can reach them.

EASY Steps — OVERFLOW CUPS

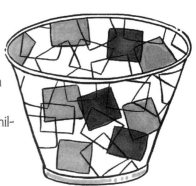

1. Give each child a cup and a cotton swab. Write the child's name on the bottom of his or her cup.

2. Let children use the cotton swabs to spread glue on the outside of their cups. Then they can press the tissue scraps to the glue in a stained-glass pattern.

3. While the cups dry, have children pour crackers into the large plastic bowl. Ask the children to guess how many crackers will fill each cup.

4. Allow children to fill their cups with crackers until the cups overflow.

PRESCHOOL CONNECTION

After children have eaten, ask for help in clearing away craft supplies and leftover crackers. Open your Bible to 2 Kings 4:1-7. Tell the Bible story in a preschool-friendly way. Ask:

· **How did Elisha help the widow?**

· **How is that like the way God helps us today?**

· **Why does God let our lives overflow with so many good things?**

Say: **God loves us and gives us good things like loving parents, a good church, friends, and healthy bodies. Our lives *overflow* with God's love! Let's thank God for his overflowing goodness.**

Lead children in a prayer, thanking God for letting our lives overflow with good things.

GOD HEALS NAAMAN
2 Kings 5:1–16

What Kids Will Do: Create pop-up Naaman puppets.

What Kids Will Need: blue plastic bowls; flat, round lollipops; white paper; crayons; scissors

Preparation Place: Use scissors to carefully make a wide slit in the bottom of each plastic bowl (similar to the slot in a child's bank). The slit should be wide enough for the lollipop to fit through. Take the wrapper off one lollipop, and trace around the candy onto a sheet of paper. Cut out two round shapes for each child.

EASY Steps POP-UP PUPPETS

1. Distribute the round papers, and let children draw Naaman's face on each one. One face should be happy, and the other should be sad and have spots on it.

2. Give each child a lollipop, and let children unwrap their candy. Demonstrate how to lick one flat side of the candy and press the round paper "face" onto the sticky surface. Let children stick one face to each side of their lollipops.

3. Give each child a prepared plastic bowl. Help children turn the bowl upside down and then poke Naaman through the hole. Children can use the pop-up puppet to show how Naaman was healed when he dipped in the water seven times.

PRESCHOOL CONNECTION

When children have finished, collect the craft supplies. Read aloud 2 Kings 5:1-16 from the Bible so children know the story is from God's Word. Then ask:

· **When Naaman was sick, who told him how to get better?**

· **When is a time you were sick? Who helped you?**

· **How did Naaman feel about God after he was healed?**

Say: **Elisha told Naaman that if he dipped himself in the river seven times, God would heal him. Elisha trusted God. We can trust God too. God has put people in our lives to help us when we're sick.**

Let each child say the name of someone who helps when he or she is sick. Then let children use their pop-up puppets to practice telling the story of how God healed Naaman.

WOWS that work
Let children add craft foam fish, green netting "seaweed," or even bits of sandpaper "mud" to the bowl to show why Naaman didn't want to dip in the water.

GOD HEALS NAAMAN
2 Kings 5:1-16

What Kids Will Do: Make washable dolls to show how God healed Naaman.

What Kids Will Need: white board Con-Tact paper, scissors, permanent markers, washable markers, wet wipes

Preparation Place: Peel off the backing from a length of white board Con-Tact paper. Fold the piece in half, so the sticky sides stick together. This will give you a piece of paper that has the white board surface on both sides. Cut several 6-inch gingerbread-man shapes from the paper. You'll need one per child.

EASY Steps — WASH-AWAY DOLLS

1. Give each child a white board person shape. Set out permanent markers, and let children draw facial features and clothes on their dolls to make Naaman.

2. Collect the permanent markers, and set out washable markers. Let children draw spots or sores on Naaman.

3. Give each child a wet wipe, and let children wash away the sores as they tell how Naaman was healed.

PRESCHOOL CONNECTION

Collect the craft supplies, and put them out of sight. Gather children in a circle on the floor for the Bible story. Read aloud 2 Kings 5:1-16, and let children act out the story with their Naaman dolls. Then ask:

- **How did God help Naaman?**
- **Why do you think God healed Naaman?**
- **How has God helped you and your family?**

Say: **God cared about Naaman, and God cares about you! God wants us to trust him, even when we're sick. God *always* cares about us. Let's sing to show that we're glad God cares for us.**

Lead children in this song, to the tune of "This Old Man."

I know God cares for me. (Hug self.)

I'm glad God will always see (hold hand above eyes)

When I'm up, down, turned around. (Jump up, squat down, turn around.)

God won't let me go! (Hug self tightly.)

I'm so glad God loves me so!

GOD HEALS NAAMAN
2 Kings 5:1–16

What Kids Will Do: Create flip pictures of Naaman.

What Kids Will Need: poster board, markers, scissors, tape, sheets of clear acetate, small stickers or paper reinforcements

Preparation Place: Cut the poster board and acetate into 6x9-inch rectangles. You'll need a piece of poster board and acetate for each child.

EASY Steps — NIFTY NAAMAN

1. Give each child a poster board rectangle, and let children draw a simple picture of a man's face.

2. Distribute the sheets of acetate, and help children tape the acetate and the poster board together at the top.

3. Let children put small circle stickers or paper reinforcements on the acetate so it looks as though the spots are on the face.

4. Demonstrate how to flip the acetate back over the poster board to reveal the face without out spots.

Permission to photocopy this box from *The Encyclopedia of Bible Crafts for Preschoolers* granted for local church use.
Copyright © Group Publishing, Inc., P.O. Box 481, Loveland, CO 80539. www.grouppublishing.com

WOWS that work

Instead of using rectangles of poster board and acetate, cut both into ovals to look like the shape of a head. Then attach a craft stick to the back of the poster board as a puppet handle.

PRESCHOOL CONNECTION

Have children help you clean up after the craft. Then gather children. Read aloud the story of how God healed Naaman from 2 Kings 5:1-16. Then ask:

• **What did Naaman look like before God healed him? What did he look like after God healed him?**

• **When is a time you were sick and God made you better?**

• **Why do you think God healed Naaman?**

Say: **God cared about Naaman, and God cares about us, too. God knows everything that happens to us, and he wants us to trust him in all situations. We can always count on God because God loves us. Before we go, let's tell God we love him, too!**

Lead children in a prayer of thanks, giving each child an opportunity to tell God that he or she loves him.

2 CHRONICLES

JEHOSHAPHAT TRUSTS GOD FOR VICTORY
2 Chronicles 20:1-30

What Kids Will Do: Make megaphones to use as they sing praises to God.

What Kids Will Need: large plastic cups, 1-yard lengths of yarn, glitter glue or paint markers, hole punch, marker, scissors

Preparation Place: Cut the bottom off of each cup. Set out all supplies on a table where children can easily reach and share them.

EASY Steps MIGHTY MEGAPHONES

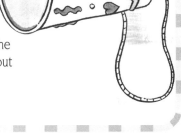

1. Give each child a "bottomless" cup, and write his or her name on it.

2. Help children use the hole punch to make one hole on each side of the smaller end of the cup (where the bottom used to be).

3. Help children slip the yarn through the holes and tie each end of the yarn to the cup.

4. Children may use glitter glue or paint markers to decorate their megaphones. When the glue or paint dries, help children slip the megaphones over their heads and use them to shout praises to God.

Permission to photocopy this box from *The Encyclopedia of Bible Crafts for Preschoolers* granted for local church use.
Copyright © Group Publishing, Inc., P.O. Box 481, Loveland, CO 80539. www.grouppublishing.com

PRESCHOOL CONNECTION

When children have finished, collect craft supplies. Read 2 Chronicles 20:1-30 aloud from an easy-to-understand Bible translation so children know the passage is in God's Word. Then ask:

· **How did God's people win the battle?**

· **How do you think God feels when he hears our praises?**

· **What are some things you can praise God for?**

Say: **Jehoshaphat and his people didn't have to fight to win the battle—they just sang and praised God! God is pleased when we praise him with singing, shouting, praying, or even whispering.**

WOWS that work

Lead children in singing into their megaphones, to the tune of "The Ants Go Marching."
The kids go praising God today—
Hurray! Hurray!
The kids go praising God today—
Hurray! Hurray!
The kids go praising God today;
We'll shout and sing and praise his name!
God will be so pleased when we
Can shout...and sing...and praise!
And sing
And praise!

JEHOSHAPHAT TRUSTS GOD FOR VICTORY

2 Chronicles 20:1-30

What Kids Will Do: Make edible flutes to remember how Jehoshaphat and his people praised God in the Temple.

What Kids Will Need: pretzel rods, frosting, M&M's candies, paper plates, wet wipes, resealable plastic bags, scissors

Preparation Place: Put the frosting into resealable plastic bags. Squeeze the frosting to one corner of the bag, then snip off that corner, creating a small hole for the frosting to come out. Set out supplies on a table where children can reach and share them. Have children wash their hands before making this snack.

Easy Steps   SWEET TWEETS

1. Give each child a paper plate and a pretzel rod.

2. Let each child squeeze about five dots of frosting along the top of the pretzel rod.

3. Instruct children to press one M&M's candy into each frosting dot, creating the flute holes.

PRESCHOOL CONNECTION

When children have finished, clean up snack supplies. Let children eat their Sweet Tweets while you read 2 Chronicles 20:1-30 aloud from an easy-to-understand Bible translation, so children know the passage is in God's Word. Then ask:

· **How did the Israelites show that they were happy?**

· **How do you show that you're happy?**

· **Why is God pleased when we praise him joyfully?**

Say: **The Bible tells us that the Israelites won a war against an army much bigger than theirs. They were very excited! To celebrate their victory, they played musical instruments to the Lord. Your Sweet Tweets are tasty reminders that it's fun to praise God.**

JOSIAH DISCOVERS GOD'S WORDS
2 Chronicles 34:1-33

What Kids Will Do: Make see-through hearts and learn that King Josiah loved and obeyed God.

What Kids Will Need: construction paper, wax paper, glue, scissors

Preparation Place: Cut two hearts from a sheet of construction paper, then cut out a heart-shape in the center to make a heart-shaped frame. You'll need one frame for each child. Tear wax paper into sheets that are a little larger than the paper hearts. Draw several crosses on a sheet of construction paper.

EASY Steps   KING JOSIAH'S HEART

1. Give each child two heart frames and two sheets of wax paper.

2. Let children spread glue on each heart shape and lay a sheet of wax paper on top of each one.

3. Guide children as they each cut out a cross. Younger preschoolers might need help with this step. Let children glue their crosses to the center of one of the sheets of wax paper.

4. Help children glue the hearts together, then trim off any excess wax paper. Point out that you can see the cross in the middle of the heart.

PRESCHOOL CONNECTION

When children have finished, have them help you clean up the craft supplies. Open your Bible to 2 Chronicles 34:1-33, and tell children the story of Josiah in your own preschool-friendly words. Then ask:

· **Josiah was only eight years old when he became king. What would it be like to be a king when you're still a little child?**

· **How did Josiah show that he followed God?**

· **What important things can you do for God?**

Say: **King Josiah must have had many decisions and choices to make at a very young age. Still, he chose to follow God and do what was right. Josiah showed that his heart belonged to God—he loved God! As you get older, you will also have more choices and decisions to make. By doing what is right, you will please God, just as King Josiah did.**

JOSIAH DISCOVERS GOD'S WORD
2 Chronicles 34:1–33

What Kids Will Do: Make eggshell reminders of the one true God we serve.

What Kids Will Need: cardboard, glue sticks, eggs, two small bowls, watercolor paints, water, cotton balls, sticky-backed magnet strip at least 1¹/₂-inches long, resealable plastic bags, needle, scissors

Preparation Place: Use a needle to poke a small hole in both ends of an egg. Hold the egg over a bowl, and blow into one hole so the egg pours out into the bowl. You will need two eggshells for each child. Refrigerate the eggs for a later use. Wash the eggshells, and set them aside to dry. Cut a 6-inch cross from cardboard for each child.

EASY Steps — EGGSHELL CROSSES

1. Give each child two eggshells and a plastic bag. Let children put the eggs into the bags, seal the bags, and crush the eggshells with their hands.

2. Distribute the cardboard crosses, and show children how to attach the magnetic backing to one side.

3. Let children turn the crosses over and cover them with glue. Then let children sprinkle the eggshells over the crosses, pressing them into the glue.

4. Have children use cotton balls to gently blot the eggshells with watercolor paint.

PRESCHOOL CONNECTION

When children have finished, have them help you clean up the craft supplies. Then gather children on the floor. Read aloud 2 Chronicles 34:1-33 from an easy-to-understand Bible translation. Then ask:

• **Why did Josiah want to follow God?**

• **How did he show that he loved and obeyed God?**

• **How can you show that you love God?**

Say: **King Josiah found that some of the people in his kingdom were praying to fake gods. The Book of the Law told King Josiah that this was wrong and that it would anger the one true God. King Josiah went through his whole kingdom and smashed the symbols to pieces, just like you crushed those eggshells! You can hang your cross magnet somewhere to help you remember that we follow only God.**

JOSIAH DISCOVERS GOD'S WORD
2 Chronicles 34:1-33

What Kids Will Do: Make books to remind them of the Book of the Law that Josiah found.

What Kids Will Need: 6x9-inch pieces of brown construction paper, plain white paper, hole punch, 14-inch pieces of yarn, scissors

Preparation Place: Cut each sheet of white paper into four equal pieces. You'll need four of these pieces per child. Set all supplies on a table where children can easily reach them.

EASY Steps

BOOK OF THE LAW

1. Give each child a piece of brown paper, and let kids crinkle up the paper and smooth it out. Children may repeat this several times. Then help children fold the paper in half to look like an old book cover. Place the white paper inside.

2. Have children hold the white paper snugly against the fold of the brown paper. Then use a hole punch to put two holes, spaced three inches apart, into the folded side.

3. Direct children to lace the yarn through the holes. Help them tie a bow on the front of the book.

PRESCHOOL CONNECTION

When children have finished, have them help you clean up the craft supplies. Then gather children on the floor. Open your Bible to 2 Chronicles 34:1-33 so children know the story is from God's Word. Then tell the story in your own preschool-friendly words. Then ask:

• **What was so special about the book Josiah found?**

• **The Book of the Law helped Josiah know how to obey God. How is that like our Bible?**

• **What other things can you learn from the Bible?**

Say: **Josiah used a special book to help his people follow and please God. We have God's Word—the Bible—to help us follow and please God today. In the books you made today, you can draw pictures of things you learn about God.**

Set out picture Bibles, and let children look through them to learn more about God. Then let children draw pictures of things they know about God or special Bible stories they remember.

NEHEMIAH

NEHEMIAH REBUILDS THE WALL
Nehemiah 2:11—6:19

What Kids Will Do: Build a cookie wall and learn how Nehemiah rebuilt a wall around Jerusalem.

What Kids Will Need: rectangular wafer cookies, paper plates, gummy bears

Preparation Place: Set out the cookies where children can easily reach them.

EASY Steps   SAFE IN GOD'S LOVE

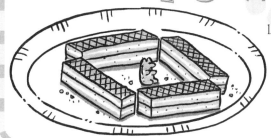

1. Give each child a plate.

2. Direct children to each set a gummy bear in the middle of their plates.

3. Have children use the cookies to build a wall around the gummy bear. Children may build the wall two "stories" high.

WOWS that work

Before children enjoy their snacks, lead them in this song to the tune of "London Bridge."

Nehemiah built a wall,
Built a wall, built a wall.
Nehemiah built a wall—
Big and tall.

All the people stayed quite safe,
Stayed quite safe, stayed quite safe.
All the people stayed quite safe
Behind the wall.

PRESCHOOL CONNECTION

When children have finished, collect craft supplies. Open your Bible to Nehemiah 2:11—6:19, and show children the passage so they know the story is in God's Word. In your own words, tell children the story of Nehemiah, who rebuilt the walls of Jerusalem. Then ask:

· **Why did Nehemiah need to make a wall around the city?**

· **How do you think the people felt, with only a broken wall to protect them?**

· **Who protects you?**

Say: **Nehemiah knew that it was important to rebuild a big wall that would go all around the city of Jerusalem. This wall protected the people, just as God can protect you. God knows you very well and wants to take good care of you. God loves you and wants you to be safe.**

NEHEMIAH REBUILDS THE WALL
Nehemiah 2:11—6:19

What Kids Will Do: Make stone coasters to remind them of the stone walls that protected the people of Jerusalem.

What Kids Will Need: plastic coasters or lids from round food containers, aquarium pebbles, paper towels, glue, marker

Preparation Place: If necessary, remove the corkboard inset from each coaster. Set out all supplies where children can easily reach them. You may want children to do this project on the floor, seated on a sheet for easy cleanup.

EASY Steps CUP COASTERS

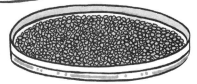

1. Give each child a coaster, and show children how to place the coaster so it looks like a shallow bowl. Let children pour glue into the coaster until the bottom is covered.

2. Have children push aquarium pebbles into the glue until the glue is completely covered. Children may search for smaller pebbles to fill in any empty spots.

3. Direct children to set their coasters on paper towels. Write each child's name on his or her paper towel. The coasters will need to dry overnight to ensure that the glue is set.

PRESCHOOL CONNECTION

When children have finished, collect crafts supplies. Open your Bible to Nehemiah 2:11—6:19, and show children the passage so they know the story is in God's Word. In your own words, tell children the story of Nehemiah, who rebuilt the walls of Jerusalem. Then ask:

• **What would it be like to build a wall made of big, heavy stones?**

• **How do you feel when you're asked to do something that seems hard?**

• **How would you feel if lots of your friends wanted to help you?**

Say: **In this Bible story, Nehemiah asked the people to rebuild a very big wall with lots and lots of stones. This was a huge job! Some of the workers got tired and wanted to quit, but because they worked together and didn't give up, all of the stones were placed and the wall was finished. If God gives us hard jobs, you can believe that he will also give the strength we need to finish them.**

WOWS *that work*

Explain that sometimes we set a cup on a coaster to protect a tabletop from water or scratches. Point out that Nehemiah built the wall to protect the people from harm too!

NEHEMIAH REBUILDS THE WALL
Nehemiah 2:11—6:19

What Kids Will Do: Make puzzles to show how Nehemiah rebuilt the gates and walls.

What Kids Will Need: jumbo craft sticks, tape, washable colored markers

Preparation Place: Set out supplies where children can easily reach them.

EASY Steps — REBUILDING THE GATES

1. Give each child seven craft sticks, and show children how to line up the sticks side by side. Help children put a piece of tape across one side to hold the sticks together, then flip them over.

2. Children may use markers to draw a gate in the shape of an "M" from the top of the sticks to the bottom. In the middle of each gate, draw a door handle.

3. Let each child remove the tape and mix up his or her pieces. Have children rebuild their gates by putting the puzzles back together.

PRESCHOOL CONNECTION

When children have finished, collect craft supplies. Open your Bible to Nehemiah 2:11–6:19, and show children the passage so they know the story is in God's Word. In your own words, tell children the story of Nehemiah, who rebuilt the walls and gates of Jerusalem. Then ask:

• **Why are gates important? What might happen if a gate was broken?**

• **Why do you think Nehemiah wanted to fix the broken gates around the city?**

• **Nehemiah wanted the city to look nice and to be a safe place. What can you do to make our church a nice, safe place to be?**

Say: **Nehemiah worked hard to make the city look new again. He wanted Jerusalem to be a special place for God's people. We can make our church a nice, safe place for God's people to be too. Let's work right now to make our room beautiful, just like Nehemiah's gates!**

Lead children in cleaning up your classroom, pushing in chairs, putting away toys, or washing dirty toys. Congratulate children on making God's house look so nice.

ESTHER

QUEEN ESTHER IS BRAVE
Esther 2:1–18; 4:1–17; 5:1–8; 7:1–10

What Kids Will Do: Create a royal scepter to remember how King Xerxes welcomed Queen Esther.

What Kids Will Need: one 2 ½-inch Styrofoam ball, one 10-inch wooden dowel, glue, ½-inch wide gold ribbon cut to various lengths, stapler, washable markers

Preparation Place: Set all supplies on a table where children can easily reach them. For younger preschoolers, you may want to push the dowel into the ball and glue it in place ahead of time.

WOWS that work

Have all children stand on one side of the room. Choose one child to be King Xerxes and stand on the other side of the room. King Xerxes may tell children how many steps to take toward him or her. The children must say, "King Xerxes, may I?" King Xerxes should hold out his or her scepter and say, "Yes, you may." As children play, remind them that Esther was glad that King Xerxes held out his scepter to her.

EASY Steps — KING XERXES' GOLDEN SCEPTER

1. Give each child a Styrofoam ball and a dowel. Help children gently push the dowel halfway into the ball and glue it in place.

2. Direct children to wrap ribbon around the ball in a crisscross pattern and secure in place with staples. Encourage children to continue wrapping until the ball is mostly covered.

3. Children may use markers to decorate the dowels.

4. Help each child tie three long pieces of ribbon to his or her scepter, where the dowel and the ball meet, so that the ribbons hang down.

PRESCHOOL CONNECTION

When children have finished, collect craft supplies. Open your Bible to Esther 2:1-18; 4:1-17; 5:1-8; 7:1-10, and show children the passage so they know the story is in God's Word. In your own words, tell children the story of Queen Esther. Then ask:

· **How would you feel if you had to go before a king?**

· **What can you do when you feel afraid?**

Say: **Queen Esther was brave. The king was a very powerful man, and she wasn't sure if the king would be nice to her. Esther asked many people to pray for her before she met with the king. God answered those prayers and kept Queen Esther from harm. We can pray when we're afraid too. God hears every prayer and will help us be brave.**

QUEEN ESTHER IS BRAVE
Esther 2:1-18; 4:1-17; 5:1-8; 7:1-10

What Kids Will Do: Use sponge stamps and ribbon to decorate a door hanger.

What Kids Will Need: paper door hangers with holes punched about 1 inch apart along the sides and bottom, 30-inch pieces of ribbon no wider than 1/4-inch, sponge stamps of hearts and crosses, paper plates, washable paint, marker, newspaper

Preparation Place: Cover a table with newspaper. Pour a thin layer of washable paint onto several paper plates, and set the plates on the newspaper.

EASY Steps — GOD IS WITH ME!

1. Give each child a door hanger and a piece of ribbon. Direct children to begin at the top of the hanger and lace the ribbon through each hole, leaving about eight inches hanging loose. Tie the ends in a bow.

2. Let each child press a cross stamp into the paint and then onto the upper portion of the hanger. Point out that the cross reminds us of God.

3. Have children do the same with the heart sponges, placing them under the stamped crosses. Explain that the heart shows how much God loves us.

4. Print the child's name under the heart stamp, then set the door hanger aside to dry.

WOWS that work

Cut a common household sponge into the shapes of hearts and crosses to make the stamps. Allow the children to practice using the stamps on newspaper before stamping their door hangers.

PRESCHOOL CONNECTION

When children have finished, collect craft supplies. Open your Bible to Esther 2:1-18; 4:1-17; 5:1-8; 7:1-10, and show children the passage so they know the story is in God's Word. In your own words, tell children the story of Esther. Then ask:

· **How do you think Esther felt before she talked to the king?**

· **What helps you feel better when you're afraid?**

· **Why does having a friend along make us feel less afraid?**

Say: **Queen Esther was afraid to go before the king, but she knew it was the right thing to do. She prayed to God, and God helped her to be brave. Even though she couldn't see him, Queen Esther knew that God was her friend and was right there with her. When you get home, place your hanger on a doorknob to remind you that, even though you can't see him, God loves you very much and is always with you!**

ESTHER SAVES GOD'S PEOPLE
Esther 8:17; 9:18–23

What Kids Will Do: Make gift bags to celebrate how Queen Esther saved her people.

What Kids Will Need: white paper lunch sacks, paper plates or pie tins, cotton swabs, tempera paint, 10-inch lengths of ribbon, individually wrapped snacks, newspaper, hole punch

Preparation Place: Cover tables with newspaper, then pour paint into paper plates or pie tins. Set out all supplies on a table where children can easily reach and share them.

EASY Steps   GOOD GIFT BAGS

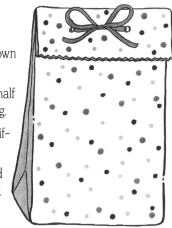

1. Give each child a white paper lunch sack. Help children fold the tops of their bags down approximately two inches.

2. Guide children in using a hole punch to make two holes, approximately an inch and a half from each side of the folded flap. Be sure the hole punch goes through all layers of the bag.

3. Let children dip cotton swabs in paint and decorate their bags by making dots of many different colors.

4. When children are happy with their designs, let them each choose an individually wrapped snack to place inside their bags. Then lace the ribbon through the holes, and tie it in a bow.

PRESCHOOL CONNECTION

Place the bags aside to dry, and ask children to help you clean up the work area. Read the story of Esther from an easy-to-understand Bible translation. Then ask:

· **Who can tell me about a gift, or present, they've** *gotten*?

· **Who can tell me about a gift, or present, they've** *given* **to someone else?**

· **Do you think it feels better to** *get* **a gift or to** *give* **a gift?**

Say: **The Bible tells us that the people gave gifts of food to one another to celebrate their joy when Esther saved them. Think of someone who makes you feel happy. You can share this special gift of food with that person, just like the Jews did in the book of Esther.**

ESTHER SAVES GOD'S PEOPLE
Esther 8:17; 9:18–23

What Kids Will Do: Make bells to celebrate Esther's triumph.

What Kids Will Need: Styrofoam cups, chenille wires, jingle bells, scissors

Preparation Place: Use a pair of scissors to make a small hole in the bottom of each cup. Set out all other supplies where children can easily reach them.

EASy Steps A CUPPLE OF BELLS

1. Give each child a cup, a chenille wire, and two jingle bells.

2. Demonstrate how to bend the wire in half and slip one jingle bell on each end of the wire. Let children twist the wire so the bells stay attached.

3. Help children push the middle section of the wire through the hole in the bottom of the cup. The bells should remain inside the cup, and a loop of chenille wire will be outside the cup.

PRESCHOOL CONNECTION

Let children assist with cleanup, then gather them. Read aloud Esther 8:17; 9:18-23 from an easy-to-understand Bible so the children know the passage is from God's Word. Then ask:

· **Why did the Jews celebrate?**

· **What are some great things God has done for us?**

· **How can you celebrate and thank God for his goodness?**

Say: **The Jews celebrated with feasting and joy! They were glad that God had sent Esther to save them from Haman. God gives us many blessings, too—families, churches, healthy bodies, and good friends. We can shake our bells as we celebrate our good God.**

Lead children in ringing their bells and shouting, "Thank you, God!"

PSALMS

THE LORD IS MY SHEPHERD
Psalm 23

What Kids Will Do: Make comforting pillows to remind them of the comfort God gives to us.

What Kids Will Need: 10x12-inch pieces of cotton fabric, tape, fast-drying fabric glue, cotton batting or fiberfill

Preparation Place: Set all supplies on a table where children can easily reach them.

EASY Steps   PILLOWS OF PEACE

1. Give each child two pieces of cotton fabric. Have them place the material flat on the table, *right sides together.* Use a piece of tape to mark one end. (This will be the end you leave open for stuffing.)

2. Direct children to lift the top piece of material and make a solid line of glue on the bottom piece of material. Then have children press the pieces together. Help children repeat this step for the other two unmarked sides.

3. Guide children to turn the material right side out, gently poke out the corners, and fill it with batting.

4. Let children remove tape from the open end. Fold the edge inside itself. Apply glue and press the material together.

PRESCHOOL CONNECTION

Set the pillows aside to dry. Let children assist with cleanup, then gather them. Read aloud Psalm 23 from an easy-to-understand Bible so the children know the passage is from God's Word. Then ask:

- **What did the shepherd do to make the sheep feel safe?**
- **Who are the people in your life that make sure you are safe and comfortable?**
- **How do you feel when you have those people near you?**

Say: **The Twenty-third Psalm tells us that God wants to comfort us, keep us safe, and give us peace. The next time you feel scared, hug your new pillow close to your heart and think about how much God loves you and likes to be near you. Let's pray and thank God for his great love for us.**

Lead children in prayer, thanking God for the comfort he gives to us.

WOWS that work
Use fabric paint to print each child's name on his or her pillow to personalize it.

113

THE LORD IS MY SHEPHERD
Psalm 23

What Kids Will Do: Design sun catcher symbols of Psalm 23.

What Kids Will Need: 16x12-inch pieces of clear Con-Tact paper, blue and green tissue paper, hole punch, 20-inch pieces of ribbon

Preparation Place: Set out all supplies on a table where children can easily reach them.

EASY Steps

SUN CATCHERS

1. Fold the pieces of Con-Tact paper in half. Starting at one corner, carefully peel the backing halfway off so that 8x12 inches of the paper is exposed. Let children tear off several large pieces of blue tissue paper. Have them stick the pieces to the sticky sides of their Con-Tact paper, forming "ponds."

2. Instruct children to tear off smaller pieces of green tissue paper to surround the pond with a green "pasture." Direct children to overlap the pieces as needed until the entire sheet is covered.

3. Help children peel off the remaining backing and fold it over the tissue paper. Punch two holes in the top, and guide children as they lace ribbon through. Tie the ends to form hangers for the sun catchers.

Permission to photocopy this box from *The Encyclopedia of Bible Crafts for Preschoolers* granted for local church use.
Copyright © Group Publishing, Inc., P.O. Box 481, Loveland, CO 80539. www.grouppublishing.com

PRESCHOOL CONNECTION

If possible, tape the sun catchers to a window, and let the children admire their handiwork while you open the Bible to Psalm 23. Read aloud verses 1 and 2. Then ask:

• **Can you think of someone who seems very busy most of the time?**

• **What kinds of things keep that person busy?**

• **How do you think that person would feel if he or she could lie down and rest in warm, soft grass next to the quiet, still waters of a pond?**

Say: **Sometimes we get very busy and forget that God wants us to be happy and live peacefully. Hang your sun catcher in a window at home to remind you that when you need rest or comfort, God is waiting.**

THE LORD IS MY SHEPHERD

Psalm 23

What Kids Will Do: Make sweet, edible sheep.

What Kids Will Need: large marshmallows, mini-marshmallows, pretzel sticks

Preparation Place: Have children wash their hands before making their craft snacks.

EASY Steps

SWEET SHEEP

1. Give each child a large marshmallow to be the sheep's body. To make the legs, let each child gently push four pretzel sticks into the rounded side of a marshmallow. Be sure children insert them at a slight angle so the sheep can stand.

2. Children will form the head by pressing three mini-marshmallows between their fingers until the marshmallows are stuck together.

3. Help children break the three remaining pretzel sticks in half and use one to attach the head to the body.

4. Children can insert one broken pretzel stick into each side of the head to make ears and one opposite the head to be the tail.

PRESCHOOL CONNECTION

Discard remaining pretzel pieces, and gather children on the floor. Ask:

· **What are some things a shepherd might do to care for his sheep?**

· **Why do shepherds do those things for the sheep?**

· **How does God take care of you?**

Open your Bible to Psalm 23, and show children the words. Say: **The Bible tells us that we are like sheep and God is our shepherd. We need someone to watch over us and take care of us. God loves us so much that he never stops watching over us. He is a good shepherd.**

WOWS that work

Let the children make several sheep to represent their families or friends. Then encourage them to pray for their "flock."

ISAIAH

ISAIAH SEES GOD'S HOLINESS
Isaiah 6:1–8

What Kids Will Do: Make angels and learn that Isaiah saw angels that were praising God.

What Kids Will Need: round slotted clothespins, white tissues, fine-tipped black pens, 3-inch lengths of white chenille wire, tacky glue

Preparation Place: Set out all materials on a table where children can easily reach them.

EASY Steps   HEAVENLY ANGELS

1. Give each child a tissue, and guide children as they tear their tissues into three equal pieces. Show children how to pinch the center of each tissue piece and slide it into the slot in the clothespin.

2. Let children use black pens to draw eyes and a mouth on the rounded end of the clothespin. (You may need to do this step for younger preschoolers.)

3. Have each child form a halo by wrapping a chenille wire around his or her finger and twisting the wire to make it stay. Kids should leave about an inch and a half straight.

4. Let children glue the halos to the backs of the angels' heads, leaving a space between the top of the head and the halo.

PRESCHOOL CONNECTION

When children have finished, collect craft supplies. While the children hold their angels, open the Bible to Isaiah 6 and read aloud verses 1-3. Then ask:

- **What were the angels in this story doing?**
- **Who was seated on the throne that the angels were flying around?**
- **How would you feel if, like Isaiah, you saw an angel with your very own eyes?**

Say: **Angels are heavenly beings and are very special. They're God's helpers! The angels helped Isaiah to be brave so that he could tell others about God's love for them.**

WOWS that work

Suspend the angel by tying a string around its neck as a reminder of the flying angels Isaiah saw.

ISAIAH SEES GOD'S HOLINESS
Isaiah 6:1-8

What Kids Will Do: Make movable Isaiahs to show that Isaiah wanted to serve God.

What Kids Will Need: plastic spoons, small rubber bands, chenille wires, pencils, tacky glue, brown or black yarn cut into short pieces for hair, small wiggly eyes, small pieces of red paper, scissors

Preparation Place: Cut the red paper into small C-shaped pieces to make mouths. For younger preschoolers, you might want to wrap rubber bands near the bottom of the spoon handles.

EASY Steps   WILLING HELPERS

1. Give each child a spoon, and help him or her wrap two chenille wires around a pencil, then stretch the wires slightly. Help children find the middle of the wires by folding them in half.

2. Let each child twist one wire tightly around the spoon, just under the bowl, to form the arms.

3. Demonstrate how to wrap the rubber band around the bottom of the spoon handle. Then let children twist the second chenille wire around the spoon, just above the rubber band. (The rubber band will help keep the chenille wire in place.)

4. Allow children to turn their spoons so the rounded sides of the bowls are facing up. Children may glue on hair, mouths, and eyes.

PRESCHOOL CONNECTION

When children have finished, collect craft supplies. Read Isaiah 6:1-8 aloud from an easy-to-understand Bible translation so children know the passage is in God's Word. Then ask:

• **What do we do in this classroom when we want to be chosen to answer a question or to volunteer for something?**

• **Do you think Isaiah raised his hand when he said, "Here I am! Send me!"?**

• **How do you think it made God feel to see Isaiah so willing to help him?**

Say: **When we volunteer to do kind things for others, it is like doing a kind thing for God. We can be like Isaiah and tell God that we want to serve him too.** Demonstrate how the Isaiah puppet can easily raise its hand. **Let's think of other ways we can serve God.**

Let children use their puppets to act out kind things they can do with their hands, arms, and legs. Children might show their puppets hugging someone, giving a gift, running to get something, or walking to church.

GOD TELLS PEOPLE TO GET READY
Isaiah 9:6; Jeremiah 33:14-16; Luke 3:7-18

What Kids Will Do: Create baby quilts to remind them to get ready for Jesus.

What Kids Will Need: 9x12-inch sheets of paper, scraps of pastel fabric, glue, marker

Preparation Place: Cut fabric scraps into 3-inch squares. Draw twelve 3-inch squares on each sheet of paper.

EASY Steps — BABY BLANKETS

1. Give each child a sheet of paper, then write each child's name on the back of his or her paper.

2. Help children set the fabric squares on the paper, in a pattern, creating a "baby quilt."

3. Let children glue their fabric squares in place.

PRESCHOOL CONNECTION

When children have finished, collect craft supplies. Open your Bible to Isaiah 9:6, and say: **In the Bible, God told a man named Isaiah that Jesus would come. He said that a baby would be born that would be Christ the Lord. Isaiah told the people to get ready for Jesus!** Then ask:

· **What do people do when they're getting ready for a baby to be born?**

· **Why does God want us to be ready for Jesus?**

· **How can we show that we're excited about Jesus?**

Say: **When people are expecting a baby, they make or buy soft blankets that can cover and warm the baby. We can get ready for Jesus by telling others about him or thanking God for sending his Son. It's exciting to know that God sent his Son, Jesus!**

WOWS that work

Use pinking shears to cut 9x12-inch pieces of flannel. Let children make their blankets on the soft flannel rather than on paper.

GOD TELLS PEOPLE TO GET READY
Isaiah 9:6; Jeremiah 33:14–16; Luke 3:7–18

What Kids Will Do: Make cards to announce that Jesus is coming.

What Kids Will Need: 4x6-inch pieces of card stock, plus matching envelopes; various small stamps (approximately smaller than 1 inch); washable stamp pads; marker

Preparation Place: Write, "Jesus is coming!" in the center of each card.

EASY Steps

AWESOME ANNOUNCEMENTS

1. Give each child a card, then write each child's name on the front of his or her card. (Older children may want to sign their own names.)

2. Let children use the stamps to decorate the envelopes and the edges of the cards.

3. Ask each child the name of someone he or she would like to tell about Jesus. Write that person's name on the front of the envelope, then let the child seal the envelope.

Permission to photocopy this box from *The Encyclopedia of Bible Crafts for Preschoolers* granted for local church use. Copyright © Group Publishing, Inc., P.O. Box 481, Loveland, CO 80539. www.grouppublishing.com

PRESCHOOL CONNECTION

When children have finished, collect craft supplies. Open your Bible to Isaiah 9:6; Jeremiah 33:14-16; Luke 3:7-18 and say: **In the Bible, God told many people that Jesus was coming. God wanted them to know that his own Son would come to take away all the bad things we've done. People were excited that Jesus was coming!** Then ask:

· **What do you do when you have exciting news to share?**

· **Who can you tell about Jesus?**

· **How can you tell others about God's Son, Jesus?**

Say: **Sometimes we send cards or letters to tell happy news. You can give these cards to special people to help them get excited about Jesus.**

DANIEL

DANIEL IS SAFE IN THE LIONS' DEN
Daniel 6:1–23

What Kids Will Do: Make praying hands as they learn that Daniel prayed to God.

What Kids Will Need: pencils, 8½x11-inch pieces of light-colored construction paper, white paper scraps, glue sticks, crayons or markers, sequins (optional)

Preparation Place: Fold each sheet of construction paper in half to make a card. You'll need one card per child. Set all other supplies on a table.

Easy Steps — PRAYING HANDS

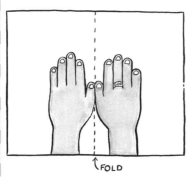

↑FOLD

1. Give each child a card, and demonstrate how to place your hand on the paper so your thumb is flush with the fold. Help children trace around their hands, with the fingers slightly apart. (Be sure to trace between their fingers, too.) Let children turn their cards over and repeat the process on the other side, tracing the opposite hand.

2. Allow children to trace over the pencil lines with dark markers or crayons.

3. Have children tear white paper into small ovals and then glue them onto the fingertips for fingernails. Children may want to draw rings and glue on a few sequins, too.

4. Have each child open his or her card and draw on the inside a picture of something that he or she can pray about. Children might draw things they're thankful for or pictures of prayer requests.

WOWS that work

Instead of drawing prayer requests, you might have each child draw a picture of someone for whom he or she will pray. Be sure to lead each child in a special prayer for that person. Then tell parents to help their children deliver the special cards as a way of letting people know they were prayed for.

PRESCHOOL CONNECTION

When children have finished, collect craft supplies. Read Daniel 6:1-23 from a preschool-friendly Bible translation. Then ask:

• **Why did Daniel keep praying to God even when he knew he might get in trouble?**

• **Why did God want Daniel to keep praying?**

• **Why is it important for us to pray today?**

Say: **When we pray, we sometimes put our hands together to help them stay quiet and still. We want to give our attention to God in a special way. Let's put our hands together in prayer and talk to God right now. We'll thank him for hearing Daniel's prayers and our prayers.**

Lead the children in prayer, thanking God for listening to us and caring about us.

DANIEL IS SAFE IN THE LION'S DEN

Daniel 6:1-23

What Kids Will Do: Create lion puppet reminders of the lions Daniel faced.

What Kids Will Need: brown lunch bags, orange construction paper, red and black markers, large wiggly eyes, glue

Preparation Place: Before children arrive, draw an 8-inch circle on each piece of orange construction paper.

EASY Steps — LION PUPPETS

1. Give each child a sheet of orange construction paper. Help children gently tear the circle shape from the paper. Guide children in folding the circle in half, then tearing a half circle from its center. This is the lion's mane.

2. Have children each set their paper sack upside down with the flap side up. Direct children to spread glue to the *flap only* and stick on the mane, leaving about a third of it below the flap.

3. Let children draw facial features on their lions' faces, including a nose, whiskers, and mouth. Children may glue on two wiggly eyes.

4. Help children tear a long, curved tail from a piece of leftover orange paper. Let them color one end black and then glue the tail to the other side of the bag.

PRESCHOOL CONNECTION

Gather up the craft supplies. Open your Bible to Daniel 6:1-23, and read the verses aloud. Then ask:

· **Who kept the lions from hurting Daniel?**

· **Why do you think God wouldn't allow the lions to hurt Daniel?**

· **How would you feel if you were surrounded by hungry lions?**

Say: **God loves each of you as much as he loves Daniel. God wants to protect you from things that hurt. You never have to feel frightened or alone, because God is watching over you, just as he watched over Daniel.**

WOWS *that work*

Use these puppets to act out the story of Daniel in the den of lions. Be sure children close their puppet mouths up tight when the angel of the Lord comes into the den!

DANIEL IS SAFE IN THE LIONS' DEN
Daniel 6:1–23

What Kids Will Do: Make prayer bracelets to remind them to pray always.

What Kids Will Need: small blue, yellow, and black pompoms; construction paper; shallow containers of glue; stapler or tape; marker; scissors

Preparation Place: Cut construction paper into 2x6-inch strips.

EASY Steps   PRAYER BRACELETS

1. Give each child a paper strip, and write his or her name on one side.

2. Let children dip and glue the pompoms to the paper strip (on the opposite side from their names). Direct children to make unique patterns as they use all three colors of pompoms.

3. Set the bracelets on a table to dry for a few minutes. When the glue has set, wrap each child's bracelet around his or her wrist, and staple or tape it in place.

Permission to photocopy this box from *The Encyclopedia of Bible Crafts for Preschoolers* granted for local church use.
Copyright © Group Publishing, Inc., P.O. Box 481, Loveland, CO 80539. www.grouppublishing.com

PRESCHOOL CONNECTION

When everyone is wearing his or her new bracelet, open your Bible to Daniel 6:1-23. Read the verses aloud, then ask:

• **Why do you think Daniel prayed three times each day?**

• **What kinds of things do you think Daniel talked to God about?**

• **If you could talk to God about anything at all, what would it be?**

Say: **When we talk to God about things in our lives, it keeps us close to him. You used three colors on your bracelets to remind you to pray three times each day. Yellow can remind you to pray in the morning, when the sun is coming up. Blue reminds us to pray in the afternoon, when the sky is bright and blue. Black helps us remember to pray at night, when the sky is dark. Praying is a good way to spend time with God. Wear your bracelet to remind you that God loves to hear your prayers.**

JONAH

JONAH
Jonah 1:1—3:10

What Kids Will Do: Make Jonah puppets and big fish backdrops.

What Kids Will Need: paper plates, blue markers, glue, permanent markers, white plastic spoons, child-safe scissors, blue construction paper

Preparation Place: Trace the tail fin shape (see margin) on sheets of blue construction paper.

EASY Steps — WHERE'S JONAH?

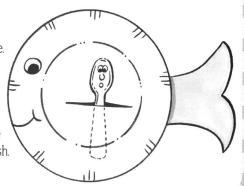

1. Give each child a paper plate. Let each child color one side of his or her plate blue.

2. Allow each child to cut out the tail fin shape and glue it to one side of the plate, creating the fish's tail.

3. Help children cut a slit in the middle of the plate.

4. Let children use a permanent marker to draw a face on the spoon to make "Jonah." Children may slip the spoon into the slit to see Jonah in the belly of the fish.

PRESCHOOL CONNECTION

When children have finished, collect craft supplies. Read Jonah 1:1—3:10 from a preschool-friendly Bible translation. Then ask:

• **Why did Jonah disobey God?**

• **How did God take care of Jonah, even when Jonah disobeyed?**

• **When is it hard for you to obey your parents and teachers?**

Say: **God had special things for Jonah to do...but Jonah didn't want to obey God. Jonah learned that it's always best to do things God's way. God wants us to obey parents, teachers, and the Bible. Use your Jonah puppet to remind someone in our class to obey God.**

Lead children in using the puppets to say, "Obey God!"

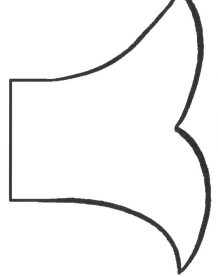

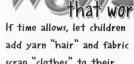

If time allows, let children add yarn "hair" and fabric scrap "clothes" to their Jonah puppets.

JONAH
Jonah 1:1—3:10

What Kids Will Do: Create snacks that remind them of Jonah and the big fish.

What Kids Will Need: blue plastic wrap, fish-shaped crackers, pretzel sticks, person-shaped gingerbread cookies, ¼-cup measuring cup, 6-inch lengths of ribbon or yarn

Preparation Place: Tear the blue plastic wrap into 12-inch squares. You'll need one square per child.

EASY Steps — JONAH'S SEA SNACKS

1. Have each child spread the plastic wrap in front of him or her to make a blue "sea."

2. Help children scoop ¼-cup of fish-shaped crackers into the center of the "sea."

3. Let children count out ten salty pretzel sticks to represent the salty sea, adding these to the pile of fish crackers.

4. Show children how to place one gingerbread person "Jonah" into the middle of the "sea." Then help children gather up the edges of the plastic wrap and form the snack into a ball. Children can hold this while you tie off the plastic wrap with a length of yarn or ribbon.

PRESCHOOL CONNECTION

When children have finished, collect craft supplies. Read Jonah 1:1–3:10 from a preschool-friendly Bible story book so children know the passage is in God's Word. Then ask:

- **What happened when Jonah disobeyed God?**
- **What happens when you disobey your parents and teachers?**
- **Why does God want us to obey?**

Say: **When Jonah disobeyed God, he found himself in the ocean, swimming with the fish! That's because God had an important job for Jonah. God sent a giant fish to swallow Jonah as a way to teach Jonah to obey. God wants us to obey our parents and teachers, too. Today give this yummy snack to someone you love, and tell that person that you want to obey God.**

WOWS that work

Get creative with this simple trail mix—add chocolate chip "rocks," mini-marshmallow "puffer fish" or any other tasty items that can remind kids of the sea!

MATTHEW

THE WISE MEN COME TO WORSHIP JESUS

Matthew 2:1–12

What Kids Will Do: Create scented sachets to remember the gifts brought to Jesus.

What Kids Will Need: cone-shaped coffee filters, spoons, bowls of potpourri, markers, ribbon (Potpourri is available in bulk at most craft stores.)

Preparation Place: Set out all supplies where children can easily reach them.

EASY Steps   SWEET SPICES

1. Give each child a coffee filter, then let children decorate the filters with washable markers.

2. Help children spoon potpourri into their filters until they are filled halfway.

3. Let children hold their filters while you tie the openings closed with ribbon.

PRESCHOOL CONNECTION

When children have finished, collect craft supplies. Read Matthew 2:1-12 from a preschool-friendly Bible translation. Then ask:

• **Why do people bring gifts to babies and children?**

• **Why did the wise men bring gifts to Jesus?**

• **How can you show that you love Jesus?**

Say: **The wise men wanted to worship Jesus and show that he was special and important. They brought gifts. Some of those gifts were spices like the ones in your little sachets! We can worship by singing, praying, or learning more about God. When you give your sweet, spicy sachet to someone, tell that person how much you love Jesus!**

Bring in gift tags, and have children tell you the name of the people to whom they'll give their sachets. Write the people's names on the tags, then attach them to the sachets. Children will love giving special gifts they've made themselves!

THE WISE MEN COME TO WORSHIP JESUS
Matthew 2:1-12

What Kids Will Do: Make tasty gift-shaped snacks to share with friends.

What Kids Will Need: graham crackers, whipped topping, colored sprinkles, red licorice whips, plastic spoons, paper plates

Preparation Place: Cut licorice whips into 3-inch strips. Set out all materials so children can reach them.

Easy Steps — GOOD GIFTS

1. Give each child a graham cracker, and have children break the cracker into two squares. Children should set each square on a plate.

2. Help children use spoons to spread whipped topping on each graham cracker square.

3. Let children shake the colored sprinkles onto the whipped topping and then place the licorice whip pieces on top in the shape of a plus sign.

PRESCHOOL CONNECTION

When children have finished, collect craft supplies. Open your Bible to Matthew 2:1-12, and show children the story. Tell the story in your own words, then ask:

- **What kinds of gifts did the wise men bring to Jesus?**
- **Why do we give gifts to people we love?**
- **What kind of gift can you give Jesus?**

Say: **The wise men came from far away to bring gifts to Jesus. They wanted to worship Jesus and show that he was special. These snacks look like little presents. Give one to a friend, and remind your friend that Jesus is a gift from God. We can worship by sharing with others and telling God how much we love him.**

WOWS that work
Drop some food coloring into the whipped topping to make your "gifts" really sparkle!

THE WISE MEN COME TO WORSHIP JESUS
Matthew 2:1–12

What Kids Will Do: Make shiny stars to remember how the wise men followed a star to find Jesus.

What Kids Will Need: 12-inch metallic gold and silver chenille wires, clear cable ties, scissors

Preparation Place: Set out all the supplies where children can easily reach them.

EASY Steps — STARS OF WONDER

1. Let each child stack six chenille wires together.

2. Show children how to wrap the cable tie around the center of the bundle and then slip the end of the tie through the small slot. Pull the tie as tight as possible so the wires are all "joined" in the center. Children can use scissors to cut the loose end of the cable tie.

3. Allow children to spread out the ends of the wires.

4. Children may cut some of the wires shorter to make more of a defined star shape. Leave one wire long, bending it into a small loop to hang the star by.

Permission to photocopy this box from *The Encyclopedia of Bible Crafts for Preschoolers* granted for local church use.
Copyright © Group Publishing, Inc., P.O. Box 481, Loveland, CO 80539. www.grouppublishing.com

PRESCHOOL CONNECTION

When children have finished, collect craft supplies. Read Matthew 2:1-12 from a preschool-friendly Bible story book so children know the passage is in God's Word. Then ask:

· **How did God show the wise men where to find Jesus?**

· **Why do you think the wise men traveled so far to find Jesus?**

· **How can we show people more about Jesus?**

Say: **God put a special star in the sky to help the wise men find Jesus. They worshipped Jesus and gave him gifts. When we are kind, talk about Jesus, sing songs about Jesus, or show God's love, others will see what Jesus is like. You can be a shining star that leads people to Jesus!**

JESUS TEACHES HIS DISCIPLES TO PRAY

Matthew 6:5-13

What Kids Will Do: Make magnetic prayer reminders.

What Kids Will Need: mini-toast (found in the deli section of most grocery stores), white poster board, tacky craft glue, magnetic strips, crayons, markers, scissors

Preparation Place: Cut a bread shape from the poster board. The shape should be ½ inch larger than the actual mini-toast. Write, "God takes care of [child's name]" around the edges of the poster board shape so the words will show after the child glues the toast in place. (You'll need one bread shape for each child, with his or her name on it.)

EASY Steps — DAILY BREAD REMINDERS

1. Give each child a piece of bread-shaped poster board. Let children color the edges of the poster board in light colors.

2. Help each child glue a magnetic strip to the back of the poster board shape.

3. Direct children to glue a piece of mini-toast to the front of the shape so that the words show around it.

PRESCHOOL CONNECTION

When children have finished, collect craft supplies. Open your Bible to Matthew 6:5-13, and show children the passage. Ask:

- **What does it mean to ask for daily bread?**
- **Why does God want to take care of our needs?**
- **Who are some people God uses to meet your needs?**

Say: **God loves us and promises to give us what we need. Jesus wanted his followers to know that they can pray and trust God to care for them. Put your magnet on your refrigerator to remember that God will always give you what you need each day.**

WOWS that work

Help children differentiate between needs and wants. Set out magazines, and look through them together. Point out fun things that we might want—like toys, books, or candy—and things we truly need—like food and water.

JESUS TEACHES HIS DISCIPLES TO PRAY

Matthew 6:5–13

What Kids Will Do: Make praying hands as they learn that Jesus taught his friends how to pray.

What Kids Will Need: self-hardening clay, plastic knives, rolling pin, wax paper, paper plates

Preparation Place: Place a piece of wax paper at each place for the children to work on.

EASY Steps — PRAYING HANDS

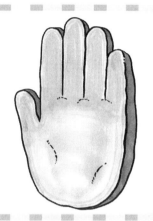

1. Direct children to each roll a fist-size lump of clay to about a half-inch thickness.

2. Have each child place one hand on his or her clay, with fingers together. Demonstrate how to use a plastic knife to trace around the hand.

3. Help each child use the knife to cut the clay on the lines around the hand shape. Remove the extra clay from the shape.

4. Set the clay hands on paper plates to harden.

PRESCHOOL CONNECTION

When children have finished, collect craft supplies. Open your Bible to Matthew 6:5-13, and show children the passage. Read the passage from an easy-to-understand Bible translation. Ask:

- **To whom did Jesus teach his friends to pray?**
- **What did Jesus want his friends to talk to God about?**
- **What do you talk to God about?**

Say: **You can talk to God about anything—God is always listening. When we pray, sometimes we fold our hands to keep them still and quiet while we talk to God. Let's practice talking to God right now!**

Guide children in folding their hands, closing their eyes, and bowing their heads. Lead children in prayer, thanking God for listening to us.

After the hands have dried, let children take them home as reminders to talk to God about everything.

WOWS that work

Give each child a pad of self-adhesive notes to glue into the palm of his or her clay hand. Families can write down prayer requests and praises on their papers each week. What a fun way to keep track of all the ways God answers our prayers!

JESUS TEACHES HIS DISCIPLES TO PRAY
Matthew 6:5–13

What Kids Will Do: Make prayer silhouettes.

What Kids Will Need: 11x14-inch sheets of black and white construction paper, gel pens, child-safe scissors, tape, glue sticks, overhead or filmstrip projector, stool

Preparation Place: Set a stool next to an empty wall away from windows. Set up the projector so the light from it will shine on the wall. For each child, tape a piece of black paper to the wall. Have the child sit on the stool with head bowed and hands folded in prayer, and have the light shine on the child, casting his or her shadow on the black paper. Use a gel pen to trace around the shadow of each child.

EASY Steps   PRAYER SILHOUETTES

1. Give each child his or her silhouette. Let children carefully cut out their traced outlines.

2. Have children cover one side of the cutout with glue.

3. Help children center the cutout and glue it onto white paper.

4. Guide children in writing their names at the bottoms of the papers.

PRESCHOOL CONNECTION

When children have finished, collect craft supplies. Open your Bible to Matthew 6:5-13, and show children the passage. Tell children the passage in your own words. Ask:

- **Who was Jesus teaching to pray?**
- **Who else can learn how to pray?**
- **What can you pray to God about?**

Say: **God is pleased when we bow our heads and talk to him. God loves to listen to you and hear what you're thinking and feeling. Let's pray in a different way right now!**

Lead children in this song prayer to the tune of "Jesus Loves Me."

P-R-A-Y every day.

God wants to hear what you say.

Thank him, praise him, know God cares.

God will answer all our prayers.

Pray in the morning.

Pray in the noontime.

Pray in the evening.

God wants to hear your prayers.

WOWS that work

This is a more challenging project that will work better for older preschoolers and pre-kindergartners.

JESUS WALKS ON WATER
Matthew 14:22-33

What Kids Will Do: Make Bible characters to use as they act out the story of Jesus walking on water.

What Kids Will Need: Styrofoam bowls, Fun-Tak or clay, drinking straws, paper, scissors, fine-tipped permanent markers, film canisters, sand, plastic tub or shallow pool of water

Preparation Place: Set out a plastic tub or shallow pool filled with water so children can take part in acting out the Bible story. Use scissors to cut a 2-inch slit into each drinking straw.

EASY Steps   FLOAT THE BOAT

1. Give each child a bowl, a straw, and two film canisters. Direct children to each cut a triangle out of paper and slip it into the slit in the straw to serve as a sail. Show children how to attach the drinking straw "mast" to a Styrofoam bowl with Fun-Tak.

2. Let children draw faces on the top of their film canisters with fine-tipped permanent markers. Children should make one of the faces Jesus and the other one a frightened Peter.

3. Help children scoop sand into the "Peter" canister, then snap the lid on tightly.

4. Let children set both canisters in the boat and act out the story from Matthew 14:22-33. Point out how Peter sinks when he takes his eyes off Jesus.

PRESCHOOL CONNECTION

When each child has had a turn to act out the story, have kids help you clean up the craft supplies. Then gather children on the floor. Ask:

· **In the Bible story, why did Peter begin to sink?**

· **What worries do you have?**

· **What did Peter do when he was afraid? What can you do when you're afraid?**

Say: **Peter was able to do something that had never been done before; he walked on water! When he took his eyes off Jesus and looked at all the scary things around him, he began to sink. Keep your eyes on Jesus when you're afraid. Jesus will help you.**

Make sure the children understand that they should never try to jump in deep water without a parent.

JESUS WALKS ON WATER
Matthew 14:22-33

What Kids Will Do: Make Peter and Jesus stick puppets.

What Kids Will Need: Styrofoam cups, wide craft sticks, crayons, sharp knife, pen

Preparation Place: Using a sharp knife, cut a slit in the bottom of each cup, about one inch across. The craft stick will slide into it.

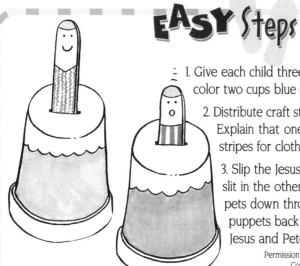

EASy Steps — PETER UP, PETER DOWN

1. Give each child three cups, and have children turn the cups upside down. Let children color two cups blue (for the sea) and the other cup brown (for the boat).

2. Distribute craft sticks, and have children draw a simple face on each stick, using a pen. Explain that one stick will be Jesus and the other will be Peter. Children may draw stripes for clothes and color them in with crayons.

3. Slip the Jesus puppet into the slit in one blue cup. Slip the Peter puppet into the slit in the other blue cup. Children may show how Peter sinks by pulling their puppets down through the slits. They can show how Jesus saved Peter by pushing the puppets back up. Slip both puppets through the slit in the brown cup to show how Jesus and Peter both got on the boat.

PRESCHOOL CONNECTION

When children have finished, have them help you clean up the craft supplies. Then gather children on the floor with their crafts. Read aloud Matthew 14:22-33, and let children act out the story with their puppets and cups. Then ask:

· **Why did Peter start to sink in the water?**

· **Sinking reminds me of getting into trouble. What kind of trouble do you get into?**

· **What can you do when you feel like you are getting into trouble?**

Say: **Peter started to get into trouble and sink when he looked around at the high waves. He shouted, "Save me, Lord!" Jesus reached out his hand and grabbed him. Jesus saved Peter.**

that work

Use fabric scraps to create clothing for the figures. Let the children wrap the fabric around the figures, securing it with glue.

JESUS WALKS ON WATER
Matthew 14:22-33

What Kids Will Do: Make waves they can walk on as they remember how Jesus saved Peter.

What Kids Will Need: brown grocery bags, blue crayons, scissors, tape or stapler, photocopies of the "Jesus" picture (p. 134)

Preparation Place: Cut off the bottom of each bag so it opens and lies flat. For younger children, draw a wavy line across the center of the bag. Set out all other supplies where children can reach them.

EASY Steps "JESUS SAVES" WAVES

1. Give each child a bag, and direct children to spread the bags horizontally in front of them. Guide each child to draw a wavy line across the center of the bag.

2. Let the children cut the bags in half lengthwise along the curvy line. Children will end up with two sections of "sea." Staple the two pieces end-to-end to make one long wave.

3. Allow children to color the waves blue. Then let children color the picture of Jesus.

4. Let children tape their pictures of Jesus to a wall. The children can lay the "water" on the floor and walk across the bag. Tell the children to try keeping their eyes on Jesus as they walk.

PRESCHOOL CONNECTION

When children have finished, have them help you clean up the craft supplies. Then gather children on the floor. Read aloud Matthew 14:22-33 from an easy-to-understand Bible translation. Then ask:

- **Who did Peter call for when he started to sink? Why?**
- **How did Jesus save Peter?**
- **When you call for Jesus to save you, what can he do?**

Say: **Jesus said, "I am here! Don't be afraid." Peter called out for Jesus saying, "Save me!" Jesus heard that cry and reached out for Peter and saved him. Jesus hears our prayers and saves us.**

WOWS that work

Teach children this song to the tune of "Frère Jacques." Children may sing the song as they walk across their waves.

"Jesus save me,"
"Jesus save me,"
Peter cried.
Peter cried.
Jesus caught and saved him,
Jesus caught and saved him.
They're safe inside,
Safe inside.

JESUS

JESUS ENTERS JERUSALEM

Matthew 21:1–11

What Kids Will Do: Make palm branches like the ones people waved to celebrate King Jesus.

What Kids Will Need: green construction paper, masking tape, child-safe scissors, paint-stirring sticks, pens, green markers or crayons

Preparation Place: Set out supplies on a table where children can easily reach them.

EASY Steps   PALM PRAISES

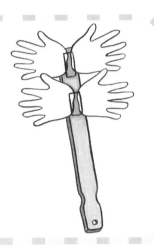

1. Distribute paint sticks, and let children color them with green markers or crayons. Encourage children to leave the handle uncolored.

2. Give each child a sheet of green construction paper. Direct children to fold their papers in half and then place their hands flat on the papers while you trace around their hands.

3. Let children cut out their handprints, creating four hand-shaped cutouts each. (Younger preschoolers might need help with this step.) Have children tape the hands to the paint sticks, with the fingers pointing out.

PRESCHOOL CONNECTION

When children have finished, collect craft supplies. Read aloud Matthew 21:1-11 from an easy-to-understand Bible translation so children know the passage is in God's Word. Then ask:

· **What did the people do to praise Jesus?**

· **Why should we praise Jesus?**

· **What can we do to show our praise to Jesus?**

Say: **Jesus is king of everything, so it was right for the people to cheer and praise him. Jesus rode a donkey that day. The donkey showed that Jesus was a king coming in peace. The people cried out, "Hosanna!" which means "save us now." Let's use our palm branches to praise Jesus right now.**

Let children stand up and gently wave their paper palms as they cheer for Jesus. Encourage each child to say something he or she knows about Jesus. Children might say, "Jesus is God's Son," "Jesus died for my sins," or "Jesus is powerful!"

Lead children in the following praise song to the tune of "Ten Little Indians."

I will praise God—
God is loving!
I will praise God—
God is loving!
I will praise God—
God is loving!
I can praise the Lord!

Let children replace the word **loving** with other words that tell about God.

JESUS ENTERS JERUSALEM
Matthew 21:1-11

What Kids Will Do: Make donkeys to remember how Jesus entered Jerusalem.

What Kids Will Need: brown paper lunch sacks, paint-stirring sticks, glue, yarn, scissors, black and white construction paper, newspaper for stuffing, scissors, large buttons or wiggly eyes, stapler

Preparation Place: For each child, cut one lunch bag in half lengthwise, fold it, and draw lines for the child to use to cut out the mane. On black construction paper, use a gel pen to draw two ear shapes and nostrils for children to cut out. On white construction paper, draw four square teeth for children to cut out.

EASY Steps — DONKEY FRIENDS

1. Give each child a whole paper lunch sack, and let him or her stuff it with newspaper to make the donkey's head. When the bag is full, gather the open end around one end of the paint stick. Let each child help you glue the open ends of his or her bag to the stick. Then tie a piece of yarn around the glued section.

2. Direct children to cut out ears, nostrils, and teeth from the construction paper. Then let children cut "fringe" from the pre-cut sections of lunch sacks to create manes.

3. Staple the ears to the tops of the bags. (The ears can be folded in before stapling to create a cupped look.) Children may glue the 3-inch pieces of yarn between the ears, as well as gluing on the button eyes, nostrils, and teeth. Then children may glue their manes to the paint stirrers.

4. Finish the donkey by tying a long piece of yarn around the stuffed bag between the eyes and nose to make the donkey's reins.

PRESCHOOL CONNECTION

When children have finished, collect craft supplies. Read Matthew 21:1-11 aloud from an easy-to-understand Bible translation so children know the passage is in God's Word.

• **Jesus said the donkey would be there, and it was! How do you think Jesus knew that the donkey would be there?**

• **What special things does Jesus know about you?**

• **What wonderful things do you know about Jesus?**

Say: **Jesus is wise and loving and knows everything about us. He knows what foods you like. He knows when you're sad, mad, and glad! Jesus wants us to know him, too. Let's take turns telling what we know about Jesus as we pray.**

Lead children in prayer, thanking Jesus for all that he is. Go around the class, and let each child say one thing he or she knows about Jesus.

WOWS that work

Let children set their Donkey Friends on one side of the room. Read aloud Matthew 21:1-7, and let children act out the story with their donkeys.

JESUS ENTERS JERUSALEM

Matthew 21:1-11

What Kids Will Do: Make confetti and candy noisemakers as they learn how people celebrated when Jesus came to Jerusalem.

What Kids Will Need: clear packing tape, crepe paper streamers, colorful candy pieces, colorful construction paper, plastic tumblers, small resealable sandwich bags, scissors, white gift bags

Preparation Place: Cut 3-foot lengths of streamers. Set out all supplies on a table where children can easily reach them.

EASY Steps — CONFETTI AND CANDY CELEBRATION

1. Give each child a tumbler, and let him or her fill it with colorful candies. Distribute three or four streamers to each child. Have each child tape one edge of each streamer just inside the lip of the tumbler.

2. Demonstrate how to turn another tumbler upside down, on top of the filled one. Let children hold the cups together while you use packing tape to tape them together. (Children will need to hold the streamers flat against the cups.)

3. Direct children to make confetti by cutting pieces of colorful paper. Then children may each fill a plastic bag with the confetti and seal it.

4. Let each child place his or her items in a gift bag. Write, "Praise Jesus Party" on the outsides of the bags.

PRESCHOOL CONNECTION

When children have finished, collect craft supplies. Read Matthew 21:12-17 aloud from an easy-to-understand Bible translation so children know the passage is in God's Word. Talk about the verse from Psalm 8:2, concerning praise coming from children. Ask:

· **How do you celebrate happy moments?**

· **How is that like the way we celebrate Jesus' love?**

· **What are some ways you think Jesus might like to be praised?**

Say: **Praise means saying good things about someone or telling how great that person is. The Bible tells people of all ages to praise God and his Son, Jesus. You can use these bags to celebrate and praise God for many, many things!**

MARK

JOHN BAPTIZES JESUS

Mark 1:4–11

What Kids Will Do: Make a dove door hanger to remember that God loves Jesus.

What Kids Will Need: yarn, hole punch, scissors, tape, poster board, photocopies of the "Dove" handout (p. 139)

Preparation Place: Wrap 6-inch squares of poster board into tubes, and staple them. You'll need one tube per child. For younger children, cut out the dove pieces from the template ahead of time. Set the tape, scissors, and templates on the table. Cut a 12-inch length of yarn for each child.

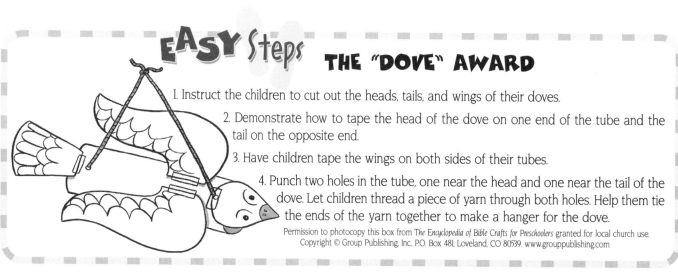

EASY Steps   THE "DOVE" AWARD

1. Instruct the children to cut out the heads, tails, and wings of their doves.

2. Demonstrate how to tape the head of the dove on one end of the tube and the tail on the opposite end.

3. Have children tape the wings on both sides of their tubes.

4. Punch two holes in the tube, one near the head and one near the tail of the dove. Let children thread a piece of yarn through both holes. Help them tie the ends of the yarn together to make a hanger for the dove.

PRESCHOOL CONNECTION

When children have finished, have them help you clean up the craft supplies. Then gather children on the floor with their doves. Open your Bible to Mark 1:4-11, and show children the words so they know the story is from God's Word. Tell the story of Jesus being baptized in your own preschool-friendly words. When you tell about God's Spirit coming upon Jesus like a dove, instruct children to hold their doves by the strings and make them "descend." Point out that God wanted everyone to know that he loved Jesus.

• **How do you think Jesus felt knowing that God loved him?**

• **How does it feel knowing that your parents love you?**

Say: **God loved Jesus and was happy that Jesus had obeyed and done the right thing. God is pleased when we do right too. Hang your dove in a place where it can remind you how much God loves you.**

DOVE

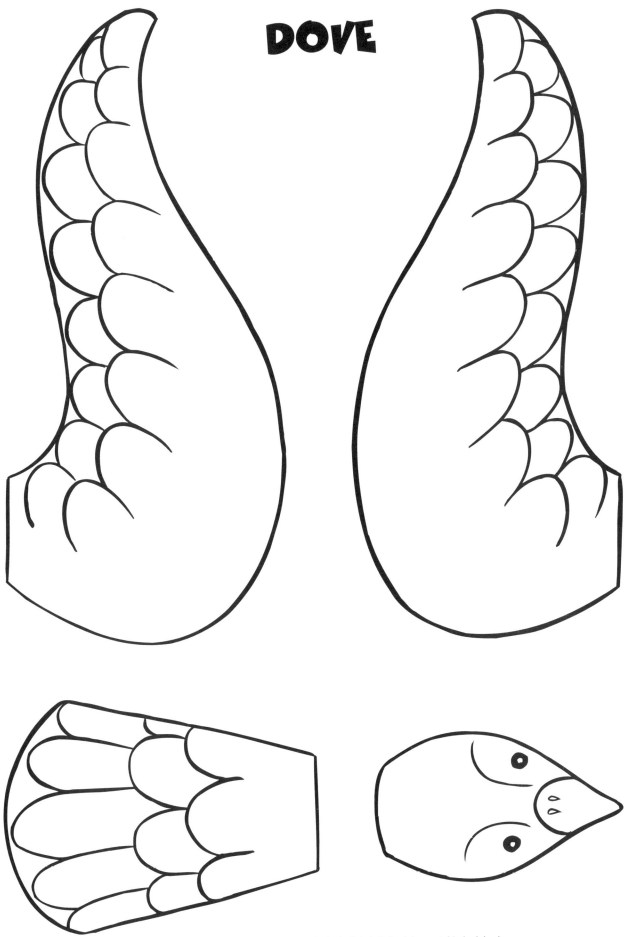

JOHN BAPTIZES JESUS

Mark 1:4–11

What Kids Will Do: Make a shoe-shaped "lacing board" to use as a reminder of John's words about Jesus.

What Kids Will Need: poster board, scissors, long shoelaces, crayons or markers, hole punch

Preparation Place: Trace around a large athletic shoe to make a simple shoe shape. Cut out one shoe shape for each child. Make a slit down the middle of each shoe, leaving the ends intact.

EASY Steps

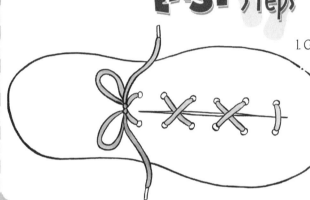

SUPER SHOES

1. Give each child a shoe shape, and write his or her name on the back.

2. Assist the children in using a hole punch to make holes along either side of the center slit.

3. Give each child a shoelace, and demonstrate how to lace the shoelace in and out of the holes. (Don't worry about what patterns children come up with as they lace.)

4. Let children decorate their shoes with markers or crayons.

PRESCHOOL CONNECTION

When children have finished, have them help you clean up the craft supplies. Then gather children on the floor. Read aloud Mark 1:4-11 so children know the story is from God's Word. Explain that John the Baptist told everyone how great Jesus was. Tell that John thought Jesus was so great that John did not think he was important enough to untie Jesus' shoes! Ask:

· **Why do you think John thought Jesus was so great?**

· **What great things do you know about Jesus?**

· **How can you tell Jesus that he's wonderful?**

Say: **John was an important helper to Jesus because John told people to get ready for Jesus and to listen to him. Jesus is great, and we can tell people all about our wonderful Jesus! When you practice lacing these super shoes, think of all the things you can tell about Jesus.**

You can reinforce the lacing holes by letting children add adhesive hole reinforcements around each one. Hole reinforcements are available at most office supply stores.

JOHN BAPTIZES JESUS
Mark 1:4–11

What Kids Will Do: Make soap balls to show that Jesus washes away the bad things we do.

What Kids Will Need: Ivory Soap flakes, shallow bowls of water, plastic sandwich bags, wax paper

Preparation Place: Set the bowls of water in the center of the table, and make a wax-paper place setting for each child. Pour about ¼ cup of soap flakes on each piece of wax paper.

EASY Steps — CLEAN-IT-UP SOAP

1. Have each child find a seat in front of a piece of wax paper.

2. Show the children how to dip their fingertips into the water and sprinkle the water on their soap flakes.

3. Let children make balls of soap by rolling the damp soap flakes in their hands.

4. Children may set their soap balls on the wax paper to dry. Once the balls are dry, transfer them into sandwich bags for easy transportation home.

PRESCHOOL CONNECTION

When children have finished, have them help you clean up the craft supplies. Then gather children on the floor. Open your Bible to Mark 1:4-11, and show children the words so they know this story is from God's Word. Talk about how John baptized people to help them know that God forgives them. Explain that John wanted people to tell God they were sorry for doing bad things. Talk about how God washes away the bad things we do, just as soap washes away dirt. Ask:

· **Why do your parents make you take a bath?**

· **How is this like what God does when we tell him we are sorry for doing wrong things?**

· **What is the best thing about knowing that God loves us?**

Say: **Soap makes you clean on the outside, but only God can make you clean on the inside. When you do wrong things, those make your heart dirty. God wants to take away all the wrong things we do so we can be clean on the inside. When we ask God to forgive us, God washes away our sins!**

By adding a few drops of cinnamon or vanilla extract to the soap flakes, you can make sweet-smelling soaps. These soaps make great gifts to send home around Christmas or Mother's Day.

JESUS CALLS THE DISCIPLES
Mark 1:14-20

What Kids Will Do: Make paintings of fish as they learn that Jesus called his disciples while they were fishing.

What Kids Will Need: scissors, sponges, several colors of bright tempera paint, liquid dish detergent, blue construction paper, sturdy paper plates, wiggly eyes, glue, black crayons, 6x9-inch pieces of wide netting, newspaper, spoons

Preparation Place: Cover the craft table with newspaper, then pour a variety of paint colors on the paper plates. Add a few drops of detergent to each plate of paint and stir. (This makes your cleanup even easier.) Use the scissors to cut the sponges into simple fish shapes. Unwrap several black crayons so children can color with the length of the crayon.

EASY Steps

FISH IN THE SEA

1. Give each child a sheet of blue construction paper, and write his or her name on it.

2. Let each child set a piece of netting *under* his or her paper and color over the paper with a black crayon. Show children how to use the wide side of the crayon. This will make the design of a fishing net on the paper.

3. Set aside the netting. Show the children how to dip a fish-sponge into the paint, wipe the excess paint on the side of the plate, and blot the sponge on the blue construction paper.

4. Have the children make fish prints until they've created schools of colorful fish on their papers. Give each child a few wiggly eyes to glue to their fish.

WOWS that work

Instead of having children color over the netting, have them glue it to the paper. Then children can paint their fish shapes on top of the netting.

PRESCHOOL CONNECTION

When children have finished, collect craft supplies. Set the fish aside to dry. Open your Bible to Mark 1:14-20, and read the passage aloud.

• **How do you think Jesus' friends felt when Jesus told them that they would go fishing for people?**

• **How do you feel when people show love to you?**

• **What are some ways you can "catch" your friends with God's love?**

Say: **Simon, Andrew, James, and John caught fish for a living. Every day they went out in a boat to catch fish with a net. Jesus told them to follow him. Jesus promised to teach them how to catch men with God's love. We can catch our friends with God's love too. When we are nice to other people, it helps them want to be friends with God, too.**

JESUS CALLS THE DISCIPLES

Mark 1:14-20

What Kids Will Do: Make "fishy" snack mix to remember that Jesus' disciples were fishermen.

What Kids Will Need: cone-style coffee filters, Swedish Fish candies, fish-shaped crackers, E.L. Fudge cookies, paper plates

Preparation Place: Set a paper plate for each child at the table. Place a coffee filter and a small pile of each of the snacks on each plate.

EASY Steps NET GAINS

1. Have children pick up their coffee filters. Explain how Jesus' friends used nets to catch fish.

2. Let the children "catch" the fish-shaped crackers and Swedish Fish on their plates and place them in their coffee-filter nets.

3. Explain that Jesus told his friends that he would teach them how to fish for people. Have the children place the E.L. Fudge cookies in their nets.

4. Thank God for the food, and let the children enjoy their yummy trail mix. Before cleaning up, let children make another "net" full of goodies to take home and share.

PRESCHOOL CONNECTION

When children have finished, collect craft supplies. Open your Bible to Mark 1:14-20, and read the passage aloud. Then ask:

· **What are some ways that God shows you his love?**

· **How can you help other people know about God's love?**

· **How do you think your friends will feel when they hear about God's love?**

Say: **Jesus wanted his friends to catch people! But they wouldn't use nets. They would "catch" people with God's love. We help people know what it's like to be a part of God's family when we treat them with kindness and love. When you share your treats with people, you'll be helping them know more about God's family!**

JESUS CALLS THE DISCIPLES
Mark 1:14–20

What Kids Will Do: Make fabulous footprints to remind themselves to follow Jesus.

What Kids Will Need: sheets of light-colored sandpaper, black tempera paint, wet wipes, paper plates, index cards, glue, marker

Preparation Place: Write, "I will follow Jesus" on one index card for each child. Pour a thin layer of paint onto the paper plates. Set supplies on a table so children can easily reach them.

EASY Steps

FABULOUS FEET!

1. Give each child a sheet of sandpaper, and write his or her name on the back.

2. Let children dip their index and middle fingers into the paint. Demonstrate how to "walk" your fingers across the sandpaper.

3. Have children make unique trails on their sandpaper. Then give each child an index card with "I will follow Jesus" written on it. Direct children to glue the cards to the sandpaper.

PRESCHOOL CONNECTION

When children have finished, collect craft supplies. Open your Bible to Mark 1:14-20, and read the passage aloud.

- **How do you think the disciples felt when Jesus said, "Follow me"?**
- **How do you feel knowing that Jesus is always with you?**
- **How can you follow the things that Jesus tells you to do?**

Say: **Jesus told the fishermen to follow him. Jesus wanted the fishermen to be his friends so he could teach them many things about God. First, the fishermen needed to leave their boats and nets so they could stay close to Jesus. Jesus is always with us, so we can stay close to Jesus too.**

WOWS that work

Give each child a large square of poster board or butcher paper. Let children take turns stepping into a plate of paint, then walking across their papers to make real footprints. Have plenty of wet wipes on hand...and foot!

JESUS HEALS A PARALYZED MAN
Mark 2:1-12

What Kids Will Do: Make a dancing man to understand how happy the paralyzed man felt to be healed.

What Kids Will Need: plastic cups, rubber bands, tape, glue, elastic string, jingle bells, paint markers, scissors

Preparation Place: Before class, cut three 8-inch pieces of elastic string per child. Set aside one-third of the pieces of elastic string. Tie one end of every remaining piece of elastic string to a jingle bell. Poke a small hole in the bottom of each cup. Set all of the supplies on the craft table.

EASY Steps FEEL LIKE DANCING!

1. Have each child take a plastic cup and set it upside down on the table. Let children use paint markers to draw a face on the side of the upside down cup.

2. Help children push the rubber band through the hole in the bottom of the cup. Direct them to tape part of the band to the inside bottom of the cup.

3. Instruct children to take two of the pieces of elastic that have jingle bells attached to them. Show the children how to make legs by taping one elastic strip to each side of the cup.

4. Have the children hold their "dancing men" by the rubber bands and make them bounce for joy.

PRESCHOOL CONNECTION

Have children help clean up the craft supplies, then gather children on the floor. Direct children to lay their dancing men on their sides. Open your Bible to Mark 2:1-12, and show children the words. Then tell the story about how Jesus healed the man who could not walk. When you get to the part where Jesus tells the man to get up and walk, have the children make their dancing men get up and move around.

- **Why do you think the man's friends worked so hard get him near Jesus?**
- **How do you think the man felt when he could walk again?**
- **What should we do when we need Jesus to help us?**

Say: **The man who couldn't walk knew that Jesus could help him. That's why he asked Jesus to make him well! We can come to Jesus when we pray—asking him to help us with our problems. Jesus always hears and answers our prayers.**

WOWS *that work*

Set out wiggly eyes and yarn, and allow children to make faces on their dancing men.

JESUS HEALS A PARALYZED MAN
Mark 2:1-12

What Kids Will Do: Make miniature pallets to remember how the man's friends brought him to Jesus.

What Kids Will Need: 3x5-inch pieces of cardboard (you can cut these pieces from a cereal box), raffia, 3x5-inch pieces of scrap fabric or felt, cotton balls, craft sticks, glue

Preparation Place: Set all of the supplies on the table within reach of the children.

EASY Steps

PALLET PRISONS

1. Give each child a piece of cardboard. Explain that they are going to be making beds like the one the paralyzed man used in today's Bible story.

2. Have children glue craft sticks to the cardboard to make handles to carry the beds.

3. Demonstrate how to glue raffia and cotton balls to the cardboard to make a soft mattress and pillow.

4. Let the children choose a piece of fabric to glue to the raffia to be a blanket for the paralyzed man.

PRESCHOOL CONNECTION

Have children help you clean up craft supplies and then gather on the floor. Read aloud Mark 2:1-12 from an easy-to-understand Bible. Explain that the man's friends had made him a special bed that they could carry wherever the man needed to go. Talk about how the man could never get out of bed until Jesus made him well.

- **What would it be like to never be able to get out of your bed?**
- **How do you think the man felt when his friends lowered him through the roof?**
- **What kinds of problems can Jesus help you with?**

Say: **The paralyzed man had wonderful friends who helped him get to Jesus. You can help your friends know more about Jesus too. Let's tell our friends about Jesus right now!**

Let children take turns telling a friend in class, "Jesus loves you!"

WOWS that work

Bring a blanket, and let children take turns lying on it while classmates pull them across the room. Talk about what it would be like to have your friends carry you everywhere.

JESUS CALMS THE STORM
Mark 4:35–41

What Kids Will Do: Make raging storms in bottles as they learn that Jesus calmed a mighty storm.

What Kids Will Need: empty plastic water bottles, blue food coloring, vegetable oil, glue, glitter, kitchen funnel, pot of water, paper cups

Preparation Place: Remove the labels from the water bottles, and thoroughly clean the bottles. Fill each bottle half-full with vegetable oil, and set them aside out of the reach of children. Set the glitter, paper cups, and pot of water on the table within reach of the children.

EASY Steps   WAVE MACHINES

1. Give each child a prepared bottle. Help each child place the funnel over the opening of his or her bottle and hold the bottle. Let each child use a cup to scoop water from the pot and pour it in the bottle.

2. Show the children how to drop a pinch of glitter into the bottle.

3. Help children squeeze a few drops of blue food coloring into their bottles.

4. Place a drop of glue on the thread of each child's bottle cap, and firmly secure the cap on the bottle.

PRESCHOOL CONNECTION

When children have finished, collect craft supplies. Open your Bible to Mark 4:35-41, and read the passage aloud. As you tell the story of how Jesus calmed the storm, have the children shake their bottles and look at the waves inside. As you finish telling the story, emphasize how the waves and wind obeyed God. Ask:

- **How do you think Jesus' friends felt when the storm obeyed God?**

- **Why it is important to obey God?**

- **What's one way you can obey God this week?**

Say: **Jesus is so powerful that even the wind and waves obey him. God wants us to obey his rules too. This week, every time you play with your wave bottle, think of a new way to obey God.**

JESUS CALMS THE STORM
Mark 4:35–41

What Kids Will Do: Make textured pictures of the disciples' boat at sea.

What Kids Will Need: paper plates, scissors, 1 pound of dry elbow macaroni, rubbing alcohol, blue food coloring, gallon-size resealable bag, cookie sheet, plastic straws, craft sticks, glue, construction paper, clear tape

Preparation Place: Several days before class, dye the macaroni blue. Fill the resealable bag half-full of noodles, and pour rubbing alcohol over them. Add several drops of blue food coloring, and seal the bag. Shake vigorously for several minutes. Carefully drain the liquid into a sink, and let noodles dry on the cookie sheet for several hours.

Cut the paper plates in half, then cut two 1-inch slits in the center of each paper plate—parallel to the straight edge of the plate-half.

EASY Steps VICTORY AT SEA

1. Give each child half of a plate and a straw. Show how to thread the straw through the two slits to make a mast. Have children use tape to secure the straw in place.

2. Have each child cut a large triangular sail from construction paper. Children may tape their sails to the straw.

3. Let children glue craft sticks across the paper plate to give the boat a woody texture.

4. Instruct children to glue blue elbow macaroni to the bottom of the boat to make waves.

PRESCHOOL CONNECTION

Open your Bible to Mark 4:35-41, and tell the story of the how Jesus calmed the storm. Ask:

· **Why wasn't Jesus afraid?**

· **How did Jesus help his friends when they were afraid?**

· **How can Jesus help you when you are afraid?**

Say: **Jesus' friends were very afraid of the storm. They thought the storm would hurt them. But Jesus wasn't afraid. He knew what to do. When you feel afraid or sad, you can trust that God always knows just what to do.**

JESUS CALMS THE STORM
Mark 4:35-41

What Kids Will Do: Make rocking boat toys to remember how the boat rocked on the stormy waves.

What Kids Will Need: empty snack-size Pringles cans, bowl of sand, roll of double-sided foam tape, card stock, packing tape, crayons, card stock, marker, child-safe scissors

Preparation Place: Before class, make two half-circle boat-shaped designs on a piece of card stock for each child. Cut the roll of double-sided tape into 1-inch pieces. Set a bowl of sand in the middle of the table.

EASY Steps · ROCKING BOATS

1. Give each child two copies of the boat shape. Have children decorate their boats with crayons and cut them out.

2. Give each child an empty can. Have children fill their cans one-third full of sand.

3. Direct children to place their lids on their cans. Secure the lids shut with packing tape. Have children lay their cans on their sides.

4. Give each child two one-inch pieces of double-sided tape. Show the children how to use the tape to fasten a boat template to each end of the can.

PRESCHOOL CONNECTION

When children have finished, collect craft supplies. Open your Bible to Mark 4:35-41, and read the passage aloud. Show children how to gently push their toy by the side of the can to make the boat rock back and forth. Explain that Jesus could make the wind and waves obey him because he was God's Son. Ask:

· **What other wonderful things do you think Jesus can do?**

· **Why can Jesus do so many special things?**

· **Why can we trust Jesus to help us?**

Say: **Sometimes our lives may feel a little like these toys—rocking back and forth. We might be afraid or confused or scared. But just as Jesus calmed the storm, Jesus can calm the storms in our hearts. Jesus can help us when we feel afraid.**

If you have a class of younger preschoolers, go ahead and cut out their boat shapes before class.

JESUS BLESSES THE CHILDREN
Mark 10:13–16

What Kids Will Do: Make a reminder that Jesus loves children.

What Kids Will Need: large paper lunch bags, 18-inch lengths of ribbon, markers or crayons, magazine or clip-art pictures, scissors

Preparation Place: Write, "Jesus Blesses [Child's name]" on each child's bag.

 **BLESSING BAGS**

1. Give each child the bag with his or her name written on it. Let children decorate the outsides of the bags with bright colors and pretty pictures.

2. Direct children to cut from magazines pictures of blessings in their lives, such as family, food, and homes.

3. Let children put the pictures in the bag, and help them tie the bags closed with ribbon.

PRESCHOOL CONNECTION

Read the story of Jesus blessing the children from Mark 10:13-16. Discuss with the children what *blessing* means and how Jesus blesses them. Ask:

• **What did Jesus do with the little children?**

• **What do you think a hug from Jesus would feel like?**

• **What wonderful things has Jesus blessed you with?**

Say: **God blesses us in so many wonderful ways! When you take your Blessing Bags home, keep adding things to them. Choose items that remind you of the way Jesus blesses you.**

JESUS BLESSES THE CHILDREN
Mark 10:13-16

What Kids Will Do: Make clocks to remember that Jesus always has time for children.

What Kids Will Need: paper plates, heavy paper, markers, crayons, paper fasteners

Preparation Place: Cut two clock hands from the heavy paper for each child. One hand should be 2x½ inches, and the other should be 3x½ inches. Make a hole in the center of the plate and in one end of both clock hands. Write the numbers 1 to 12 on the edge of the plate and "Jesus has time for ME!" in the center of each plate.

EASY Steps   ALL THE TIME

1. Give each child a plate, and read the words on the clock aloud. Let children color the plates in bright colors.

2. Guide children to color over the numbers and the words on their clocks in contrasting colors.

3. Help children attach the clock hands to their clocks using paper fasteners.

4. Show children how to turn the clock hands to make different times.

Permission to photocopy this box from *The Encyclopedia of Bible Crafts for Preschoolers* granted for local church use.
Copyright © Group Publishing, Inc., P.O. Box 481, Loveland, CO 80539. www.grouppublishing.com

PRESCHOOL CONNECTION

When children have finished, collect craft supplies. Open your Bible to Mark 10:13-16, and read the passage aloud. Then ask:

· **Why did people want Jesus to bless their children?**

· **What did Jesus' friends think about him being with little children?**

· **What did Jesus think about being with little children?**

Have the children put the hands of the clock into different places that would show times that are meaningful to them, such as 8:00 (time to wake up) or 12:00 (time to eat lunch). Point out that Jesus always has time to be with us.

Since younger preschoolers might have a hard time with the concept of time, let them cut pictures from magazines. Help children choose pictures that show things they might do—children playing with friends, eating, sleeping, playing outside, or reading. Allow children to glue the pictures to the clock instead of adding numbers. They can make the clock hands point to the things they like to do and remember that Jesus is with them all the time.

JESUS BLESSES THE CHILDREN
Mark 10:13-16

What Kids Will Do: Make toys that show how Jesus welcomed the children.

What Kids Will Need: wooden spoon about 6 inches long, small wooden ice cream spoons, tacky craft glue, markers, construction paper, scissors

Preparation Place: Make triangles from 8½x11-inch construction paper by first making an 8½-inch square and then cutting each square in half corner to corner. Set out all supplies where children can easily reach them.

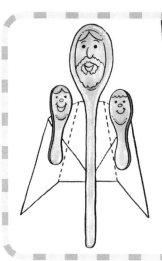

EASY Steps HUGS FROM JESUS

1. Let children use markers to draw happy Jesus faces on the bowls of the large spoons. Then let each child draw the faces of happy children on the bowls of two or three wooden ice cream spoons.

2. Give each child a paper triangle. Demonstrate how to fold down the point that is opposite the longest edge.

3. Let children fold the remaining sides of the paper triangle in to the center to form a robe. Help them glue the large wooden spoon inside the robe so Jesus' face is showing.

4. Have children glue the smaller spoon "children" to the inside of the robe.

PRESCHOOL CONNECTION

When children have finished, collect craft supplies. Open your Bible to Mark 10:13-16, and read the passage aloud. Have each child act out the story by first opening the robes on Jesus so no "spoon children" show. Then children can fold the robes closed to show the children with Jesus. Ask:

• **Who wanted to keep the children away from Jesus?**

• **What did Jesus want?**

• **What would it be like to be hugged by Jesus?**

Say: **Jesus loved children very much. He knew that they were special, just as each of you is special. Jesus didn't want to send children away. Jesus wanted to welcome and bless the children. Let's thank Jesus for loving children so much.**

Lead children in a simple prayer, thanking God for his special love for children.

JESUS HEALS THE BLIND MAN
Mark 10:46–52

What Kids Will Do: Make special glasses to discover what it might be like to be blind.

What Kids Will Need: children's sunglasses, white paper, glue, markers, scissors

Preparation Place: Cut the white paper into 2-inch circles. Set all supplies out where children can easily reach them.

EASY Steps   WIDE-EYED GLASSES

1. Give each child a pair of sunglasses and two paper circles.

2. Let children draw eyes on the white circles, making each circle into one "eyeball."

3. Direct children to glue one eyeball to each lens on their sunglasses.

PRESCHOOL CONNECTION

Let children wear their glasses and discover how hard it is to see. Then gather children, and read aloud Mark 10:46-52 from an easy-to-understand Bible translation. Ask:

· **What do you think it would be like to be blind?**

· **Tell us about a problem you had that you could not solve.**

· **How does God help us with our problems?**

Say: **Bartimaeus had a problem—he couldn't see! But Bartimaeus knew that Jesus could heal him, so he asked Jesus. Jesus wants us to come to him with our problems, too. Whether you're sad, mad, scared, or worried, God is always waiting to help!**

JESUS HEALS THE BLIND MAN
Mark 10:46–52

What Kids Will Do: Make faces that are blind but then "see."

What Kids Will Need: paper plates, razor knife, crayons, scissors, white construction paper, colored construction paper, glue, scissors, crayons

Preparation Place: Cut the white construction paper into 3x8-inch strips. Using the razor knife, cut two 3½-inch vertical lines near the top of each plate. The lines should be about 4 inches apart.

EASY Steps EYES THAT SEE!

1. Give each child a paper plate and a piece of white construction paper. Show the children how to thread the construction paper through the two slits in the plate.

2. Have the children draw a pair of eyes on the paper that is visible between the two slits. Direct them to pull the strip so the eyes don't show, then draw two half circles, representing closed eyes.

3. Each child may tear pieces of construction paper in the shapes of a nose and a mouth and glue them to the plate.

4. Show the children how to pull the construction paper side to side to hide the eyes and make them reappear.

PRESCHOOL CONNECTION

Have children help you clean up craft supplies, then gather children on the floor. Read aloud Mark 10:46-52 from an easy-to-understand Bible translation. As the children listen to the story, instruct them to adjust the strips on their plate faces to make Bartimaeus see at the appropriate time. Ask:

• **Why do you think Jesus healed Bartimaeus?**

• **Why does Jesus want to help us with our problems?**

• **How can you thank Jesus for loving you?**

Say: **Bartimaeus was so thankful that he followed Jesus! We can thank Jesus for his love in so many wonderful ways. You can pray, sing, clap, shout, or whisper your thanks to Jesus. Let's thank Jesus right now with a prayer.**

Lead children in prayer, thanking Jesus for his love.

JESUS NOTICES A WIDOW'S GIVING

Mark 12:41-44

What Kids Will Do: Make coins as reminders that the widow gave all she had.

What Kids Will Need: poster board, aluminum foil, coins, pencils, scissors

Preparation Place: Cut two poster board circles, approximately 2 inches in diameter, for each child. Set out a variety of real coins, along with the pencils and 4-inch squares of foil.

EASy Steps — THE WIDOW'S COINS

1. Encourage children to look at the different pictures and writing on the coins.

2. Give each child two poster board circles. Let children wrap each coin in a foil square, pressing the foil tightly around the poster board.

3. Direct children to use pencils to make their own unique designs on the "coins."

PRESCHOOL CONNECTION

When children have finished, collect craft supplies. Open your Bible to Mark 12:41-44, and show children the passage. Tell children the story in your own words. Then ask:

- **What did the widow have to give?**
- **Why did the widow give all she had to God?**
- **What do you have to give to God?**

Say: **The widow didn't have much to give to the church, but she gave all she could. You may not have a lot of money to give, but you can give other things! You can give your kindness or friendship to other children at church. You can give your worship and prayer to God. God wants us to give all we have, no matter how much it is!**

WOWS that work

Wrap a shoe box in brown paper, then cut a slit in the lid. Place the box in the middle of your circle, and let children come forward and put their coins in the box. As children do, have them each tell one thing they can give to God, such as their love, their time, or their prayers. Then distribute chocolate coins, and tell children that their gifts are special to God.

JESUS NOTICES A WIDOW'S GIVING
Mark 12:41-44

What Kids Will Do: Make hand reminders about loving God.

What Kids Will Need: craft foam, plastic coins, markers, scissors, glue, magnets

Preparation Place: Cut the foam into rectangles large enough for a child's hand to be traced on them.

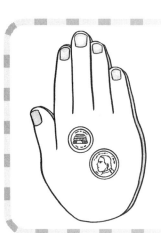

EASY Steps LOVING HANDS

1. Give each child a piece of craft foam. Help each child trace one of his or her hands on the foam.

2. Let children cut out the hand shape. Younger preschoolers may need assistance with this step.

3. Have children use markers to draw fingernails on their hand shapes.

4. Children may each glue two coins on the hand shapes. Then direct children to turn the hands over and glue magnets on the back.

PRESCHOOL CONNECTION

When children have finished, collect craft supplies. Open your Bible to Mark 12:41-44, and read the story to children. Talk about what it might have been like to be a poor widow in those days. Ask:

· **What did Jesus notice the woman doing?**

· **Why was the woman giving her two coins to God?**

· **How can you show God that you love him?**

Say: **One way we show our love to God is by giving our money and other things that are special to us. You can show your love to God by giving a special toy to a child who doesn't have any. Or you might give some of your birthday money to the church. Jesus was pleased when the woman gave all she had, and God is pleased when we give to him too.**

LUKE

JESUS IS BORN
Luke 1:26–45; 2:1–20

What Kids Will Do: Make colorful washcloths to show that Jesus came to wash away our sins.

What Kids Will Need: white washcloths, fabric paint in a variety of colors, paper plates, permanent marker, paper, pen, soap, water

Preparation Place: Pour a small amount of each color of paint onto a separate paper plate. On slips of paper, copy the instructions from the fabric paint so parents will know how to set the paint.

EASY Steps

WASH-AWAY WASHCLOTHS

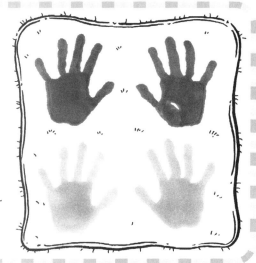

1. Give each child a washcloth, and spread the cloth flat in front of the child. Use a permanent marker to write the child's name on the washcloth label.

2. Help each child press one palm into the paint and then press the palm flat on the washcloth.

3. Let children make several handprints with each hand, washing hands with soap and water between colors.

4. Help children wash their hands thoroughly, then set the washcloths in an out-of-the-way area to dry.

PRESCHOOL CONNECTION

When children have finished, collect craft supplies. Open your Bible to Luke 1:26–45; 2:1–20. Show children the passage, and tell children the Christmas story in your own words. Then ask:

· **Why do you think God sent Jesus to earth?**

· **Why does God want to take our sins away?**

· **How can you thank God for sending Jesus?**

Say: **God loves us so much that he sent Jesus to earth to take away all the wrong things we do. When you use your washcloth, you can remember that Jesus will wash away our sins so we can be close to God.**

Teach children this song so they can sing it when they use their washcloths at home. Sing to the tune of "Row, Row, Row Your Boat."

Wash, wash, wash away.
Make me clean and new.
Jesus washes all my sins.
God loves me and you!

JESUS IS BORN
Luke 1:26–45; 2:1–20

What Kids Will Do: Use lace and handprints to make angels.

What Kids Will Need: blue construction paper, lace doilies, white paint, markers, white paper, paper plates, scissors

Preparation Place: Cut the white paper into 3-inch circles. Cut the doilies into pie-shaped quarters. Pour a thin layer of white paint into several paper plates.

EASY Steps   ANNOUNCING ANGELS

1. Give each child a quarter of a doily and a sheet of blue paper. Have the child glue the doily to the center of the paper, with the pointed side up.

2. Let each child decorate a paper circle to look like the face of an angel. Glue the angel's face to the pointed end of the doily.

3. Help children press their palms into the white paint and then press their palms next to the doilies to create the angel's wings.

4. Write, "Jesus is born!" on each child's paper.

PRESCHOOL CONNECTION

When children have finished, collect craft supplies and set the angels aside to dry. Open your Bible to Luke 1:26-45; 2:1-20. Show children the passage, and tell children the Christmas story in your own words. Then ask:

- **What good news did the angels tell the shepherds?**
- **What good news do you know about Jesus?**
- **Who can you tell about Jesus' birth?**

Say: **God sent angels to tell shepherds about Jesus' birth. The angels sang and praised God—they were happy to know that God's Son was born! We can spread the good news of Jesus' birth with lots of friends and family. Let's praise God and sing like the angels did.**

Close by singing a Christmas song, such as "Joy to the World!"

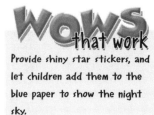

Provide shiny star stickers, and let children add them to the blue paper to show the night sky.

JESUS IS BORN
Luke 1:26-45; 2:1-20

What Kids Will Do: Make door decorations to celebrate Jesus' birth.

What Kids Will Need: large jingle bells, 2-foot lengths of wide red ribbon, craft foam shapes (angels or stars), craft glue, marker

Preparation Place: Set out all materials where children can reach them.

EASY Steps

GOOD NEWS CHIMES

1. Give each child a length of ribbon and a jingle bell. Write each child's name on the back of his or her ribbon.

2. Let children thread their ribbons through the holes in the jingle bells.

3. Help each child tie the ends of the ribbon together, creating a large circle of ribbon.

4. Direct children to glue the craft foam shapes to the ribbons.

PRESCHOOL CONNECTION

When children have finished, collect craft supplies. Open your Bible to Luke 1:26-45; 2:1-20. Show children the passage and tell children the Christmas story in your own words. Then ask:

· **When do people ring bells?**

· **How did God let the world know that his Son had been born?**

· **How can you tell people the good news about Jesus?**

Say: **Angels sang the exciting news to shepherds. The shepherds ran to tell everyone that Jesus was born. You can hang these bells on your front door. When people come in, the bell will jingle, reminding you to share the wonderful news of Jesus' birth!**

Use thick, velvety ribbon to make these door decorations even more special!

JESUS GROWS UP
Luke 2:39–52

What Kids Will Do: Make Jesus figures that grow taller.

What Kids Will Need: plastic tumblers, table tennis balls, fine-tipped permanent markers, water, newspaper

Preparation Place: Cover a table with newspaper. Set fine-tipped permanent markers on the table where the children can reach them. Fill half of the tumblers half-full with water, and set them aside.

EASY Steps

TALLER AND TALLER

1. Give each child a table tennis ball, and have kids sit at the table.

2. Show the children how to draw Jesus' face on a table tennis ball and then place the ball in an empty tumbler.

3. Give each child one of the tumblers half-filled with water. Demonstrate how to slowly pour the water into the tumbler containing the ball and watch the face rise higher and higher.

4. Talk about how Jesus was a child who grew bigger and bigger, just as they are.

PRESCHOOL CONNECTION

Let children play with their crafts for a few minutes. Then pour the water into a sink, and set the crafts aside. Gather children and read aloud Luke 2:39-52. Point out that these verses mean that Jesus was a little boy who grew up just like they are. Then ask:

· **What is the best part of growing up?**

· **Why should we keep learning about God as we grow?**

· **How can we learn about God?**

Say: **Jesus was born as a baby and grew into a little boy. Then he grew into a bigger boy, and then a man! As you grow, it's important to learn more and more about God. We can learn from our parents, from our church teachers, and by looking into the Bible. You can learn about God every day while you grow.**

You can help younger preschoolers fill their cups with water by giving them a turkey baster filled with water and letting them squirt it into the bottoms of the cups.

JESUS GROWS UP
Luke 2:39-52

What Kids Will Do: Make yummy churches filled with people who are growing in God.

What Kids Will Need: graham crackers, plastic knives, paper plates, frosting, E.L. Fudge cookies, plastic wrap

Preparation Place: For each child, set a plastic knife, a graham cracker sheet (2 squares), and several E.L. Fudge cookies on a paper plate at the table. Open the container of frosting, and set it where children can easily reach.

EASY Steps   GROWING IN GOD'S HOUSE

1. Help children break their graham crackers into two squares.

2. Let children spread frosting on one side of each cracker.

3. Guide children as they lean the tops of the graham crackers together to form "tents." Explain that these are like little churches.

4. Let children "walk" E.L. Fudge cookies inside the churches. Cover each plate with plastic wrap, and let children take their snacks home.

PRESCHOOL CONNECTION

Open your Bible to Luke 2:39-52. Say: **In our Bible story, Jesus was still a boy. He went to God's house to listen to teachers talk about God. Jesus listened, and he asked questions to learn more about God. Jesus loved to be in God's house.** Ask:

· **What would you like to learn about God?**

· **Who can you ask when you have questions about God?**

· **What's your favorite thing that you know about God?**

Say: **God is awesome. It's great to learn about him. We can go to church and learn about God—just like Jesus!**

JESUS IS TEMPTED
Luke 4:1–13

What Kids Will Do: Make heads that say "no."

What Kids Will Need: 12-inch wooden dowels, paper plates, construction paper, scissors, glue sticks, masking tape, yarn or raffia

Preparation Place: Cut out several shapes from the construction paper to be "face parts"—triangles for noses, circles for eyes, half-circles for ears, and crescents for mouths. (Be sure to cut these facial features at a size proportional to your paper plates.)

EASY Steps   "NO WAY" FACES

1. Give each child a paper plate. Encourage children to choose the shapes they would like to use to make faces on their paper plates.

2. Instruct the children to glue their shapes to the paper plates, creating unique faces.

3. Let children glue raffia or yarn "hair" to the plate.

4. Help children tape a wooden dowel to the backside of each paper plate.

WOWS that work

You can use the "No Way" Faces to practice saying no to temptation. Ask children if they want to give in to certain temptations. For example, you might say, "Do you want to take a cookie when Mom isn't watching?" The kids can shout back, "No way!" and shake their "No Way" Faces in a "no" motion.

PRESCHOOL CONNECTION

Have children help clean up craft supplies. Then gather children on the floor. Open your Bible to Luke 4:1-13, and show children the words. Using preschool-friendly words, tell the story of Jesus being tempted. Ask:

• **How do you think Jesus felt when Satan tried to trick him?**

• **Have your ever wanted to do something you knew was wrong?**

• **What can you do when you want to do something you know is wrong?**

Say: **Jesus went through a hard time when Satan tempted him. Jesus used God's Word to say no to Satan. God wants us to say no when we're tempted to do the wrong things too. Let's practice saying no so we can do what's right.**

Show the children how to hold their craft faces by the dowel, holding the dowel between their flattened palms. Children can move their hands back and forth to roll the dowel and shake the heads in a "no" motion.

JESUS IS TEMPTED
Luke 4:1–13

What Kids Will Do: Make magnetic games to remind them that they can turn to God's Word when they're tempted.

What Kids Will Need: large freezer bags, sheets of sandpaper, card stock copies of the "Bible" and "Jesus" templates at the bottom of the page, roll of magnetic strips, classroom glue, super glue, scissors, tape

Preparation Place: Cut out the pictures of the Bible and Jesus from the card stock. Cut the magnetic stripping into ½-inch pieces, and super glue the pieces to the backs of the Jesus figures. Trim the sandpaper so it fits inside the freezer bags.

EASY Steps — TEMPTATION PUSHERS

1. Give each child a freezer bag and a sheet of sandpaper. Talk about how Jesus went through a hard time in the sandy desert.

2. Help children glue their Bible pictures somewhere on their sandpaper. Then let children put the sandpaper into the bags and set "Jesus" inside too. Tape the bags shut.

4. Give each child a magnet. Show the children how to move Jesus toward the Bible.

PRESCHOOL CONNECTION

Open your Bible to Luke 4:1-13. In simple language, tell the story of how Satan tempted Jesus to do many wrong things. Explain that Jesus remembered what God said in his Word, so he knew the right thing to do. Ask:

· **What did Jesus do to stop Satan's tricks?**

· **How can knowing what God says in the Bible help you say "no" to Satan's tricks?**

· **How can you learn God's words?**

Say: **Satan wanted Jesus to do some things that weren't right. But Jesus turned away from Satan by using God's Word. God's Word helped Jesus do what was right. We can use the Bible to help us do the right things too!**

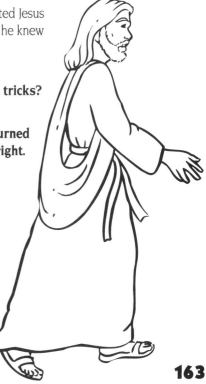

JESUS TELLS ABOUT A GOOD SAMARITAN

Luke 10:25-37

What Kids Will Do: Make special snacks that they can share to show God's love.

What Kids Will Need: sandwich bags with twist ties; trail mix that includes raisins, M&M's-type candies, pretzel sticks, and round puff cereal (such as Kix); poster board; pink construction paper; photocopies of poem (at bottom of page); hole punch; yarn; scissors; pencils

Preparation Place: Make several 6-inch poster board hearts for children to use as stencils. Cut the yarn into 12-inch lengths. Photocopy the poem "Love Your Neighbors."

EASY Steps — LOVE TO GIVE

Love Your Neighbors
All colors, all ages, short and tall;
All sizes, both big and small;
Love your neighbors;
Love them all.

1. Give each child a sandwich bag, and let children fill the bags with trail mix. Point out that the candies remind us that people come in many different colors. The raisins remind us that some people are older, with wrinkly skin. Tell children that pretzel sticks show us that some people are tall, while the cereal shows us that some people are shorter.

2. Distribute heart stencils. Help each child trace and cut out a heart from the pink construction paper. Children may glue the poems to the hearts.

3. Punch a hole in each pink heart, and let children pull the yarn through the holes. Help children tie the yarn around the bags.

4. Write, "I love you" on their hearts before they give them away to special people.

WOWS that work

Teach children this action rhyme:

I can't send a gift to God (hold out arms, as if giving a present)

To show him all my love. (Hug self.)

But here is something I can do (point to self)

While God watches from above. (Hold hand above eyes, as if looking down.)

I can love you and help you out. (Point to a friend.)

That's what love is all about. (Extend arms to side.)

PRESCHOOL CONNECTION

When children have finished, collect craft supplies. Read Luke 10:25-37 from an easy-to-understand Bible translation. Then ask:

· **How did the man show kindness to the hurt man?**

· **How can you show kindness to people around you?**

· **Why does God want us to be kind to our neighbors?**

Say: **Neighbors are not only the people who live next to us but also everyone we meet. Jesus wants us to love everyone. You can give your special snack to someone as a way of showing God's love!**

Love Your Neighbors

All colors, all ages, short and tall;

All sizes, both big and small;

Love your neighbors;

Love them all.

JESUS TELLS ABOUT A GOOD SAMARITAN

Luke 10:25–37

What Kids Will Do: Make modeling-dough figures of the Bible story characters.

What Kids Will Need: light- and dark-colored modeling dough, wiggly eyes, facial tissues, paper plates, colored napkins

Preparation Place: Set out all materials where children can easily reach them.

EASY Steps — MODELING DOUGH PEOPLE

1. Give each child a paper plate and a handful of light-colored modeling dough. Have each child form his or her dough into a ball and then form a "snake" from it. Children may flatten the snakes on the plates to make roads.

2. Distribute two handfuls of dark-colored dough to each child. Let each child form one handful of dough into the shape of a person (the traveler). Allow each child to push two wiggly eyes into the man and then wrap a facial tissue "robe" around him.

3. Let each child form another figure from the other piece of dough. Kids can add wiggly eyes and napkins for headpieces or robes.

PRESCHOOL CONNECTION

When children have finished, collect craft supplies. Open your Bible to Luke 10:25-37, and show children the passage. Tell children the story in your own words. Let children use their figures to act out the story. Then ask:

- **What did the Samaritan do for the hurt man?**
- **What can you do to help other people?**
- **How can loving others be like loving God?**

Say: **Jesus told this story to help people know that they should be loving to all people, not just to their friends. It's easy to be kind to people we like, but it's harder to be kind to people we don't like. Use your dough people to act out the story, and remember to be kind and loving to everyone.**

You may want to provide large resealable bags so children can take their figures home and keep the dough soft.

JESUS TELLS ABOUT A GOOD SAMARITAN
Luke 10:25–37

What Kids Will Do: Make "I Care" Kits for sick children.

What Kids Will Need: white paper lunch sacks, card stock, crayons, self-adhesive bandages, child-safe scissors, lollipops, stickers, markers, hole punch, string

Preparation Place: To make tracing circles easier for younger children, collect canning lids or masking tape rolls. Tracing inside a circle is easier than tracing around the outside.

EASY Steps   "I CARE" KITS

1. Give each child a piece of card stock, a lid, a pencil, and a pair of child-safe scissors. Let each child trace and cut out three circles. Punch a hole in one side of each circle, and let children slip pieces of string through the holes. Tie the string to the paper so it looks like a balloon on a string.

2. Direct children to color the "balloons" in bright colors. Older children may want to write words such as "Get well" or "Smile" on the balloons.

3. Distribute paper lunch sacks, and let children decorate their sacks with stickers and drawings. Older children may write, "I Care" on the bags.

4. Have each child fill his or her bag with the paper balloons, a few crayons, bandages, and lollipops.

PRESCHOOL CONNECTION

When children have finished, collect craft supplies. Open your Bible to Luke 10:25-37, and show children the passage. Tell children the story in your own words. Ask:

- **Why did the Samaritan help the hurt man?**
- **When has someone helped you?**
- **How can you help children who are sick?**

Say: **When people get sick, we can show God's love for them in many ways. You might bring someone a coloring book or draw a special picture. You can even call sick friends to tell them you hope they'll feel better soon. One important way to help sick people is to pray for them. Let's do that right now.**

Lead children in praying for any sick or hurt classmates, relatives, or neighbors. Children may take "I Care" Kits to give to people who are home sick. Keep the rest of the kits handy in class. When you hear of a sick child, send an "I Care" Kit for the child to have some quiet play.

JESUS TELLS THE PARABLE OF THE LOST SON

Luke 15:11–32

What Kids Will Do: Make puffy pigs to remember the pigs that the lost son had to feed.

What Kids Will Need: 1-inch pink pompoms, ½-inch pink pompoms, ¼-inch pink pompoms, ⅛-inch pink pompoms, wiggly craft eyes, 3-inch pieces of pink chenille wire, tacky craft glue, paper plates, pencil

Preparation Place: Wind each pink chenille wire around a pencil to make a curly tail. Pour craft glue onto paper plates so children can dip their pompoms into it. Set out all materials where children can easily reach them.

EASY Steps   POMPOM PIGS

1. Give each child a large pompom, and explain that this is the pig's body. Direct children to each glue four ¼-inch pompoms onto the large pompoms as legs.

2. Let each child glue two wiggly eyes onto a ½-inch pompom to create the pig's head.

3. Have children glue the heads onto the bodies of their pigs.

4. Allow children to glue curly pick chenille wires onto the backs of the bodies as tails.

PRESCHOOL CONNECTION

When children have finished, collect craft supplies. Open your Bible to Luke 15:11-32, and show children the passage. Tell children the parable of the prodigal son in your own words. Ask:

· **Where did the younger son go?**

· **Why did the son have to feed pigs?**

· **How did the father feel about the son coming back home?**

Have children take their pigs home as reminders that God loves us, no matter where we have been or what we have done.

JESUS TELLS THE PARABLE OF THE LOST SON
Luke 15:11-32

What Kids Will Do: Make festive party hats as they learn how the father rejoiced when his son returned.

What Kids Will Need: paper plates, scissors, crayons, markers, stickers, hole punch, tape, yarn

Preparation Place: Cut a pie shape from each paper plate so that you can fold the plates into a wide cone shape. Punch a hole on each side of the plate so you can add yarn to tie on the hat.

EASY Steps   PARTY HATS

1. Give each child a paper plate that you've cut. Let children decorate the paper plates as if for a party.

2. Help children fold the plates into cone shapes and tape them securely.

3. Guide children to slip a piece of yarn through each hole and tape the yarn in place.

4. Let children put on their hats. Tie the yarn loosely under each child's chin.

PRESCHOOL CONNECTION

When children have finished, collect craft supplies. Open your Bible to Luke 15:11-32, and show children the passage. Read the passage from an easy-to-understand Bible translation. Ask:

· **How do you think the father felt when his younger son left home?**

· **When the son ran out of money, what did he decide to do?**

· **How did the father feel when the son returned home?**

· **What did the father do to show how happy he was?**

Say: **The father was so happy when his son came home that he threw a big party! God is like the father in this story. God is so happy when we come to him and make Jesus our forever friend. Take your hats home, and remember that God celebrates when we love him.**

JESUS TELLS THE PARABLE OF THE LOST SON

Luke 15:11-32

What Kids Will Do: Make special rings like the father might have given to the son.

What Kids Will Need: chenille wires, large beads, scissors

Preparation Place: Cut the chenille wires into 2-inch segments, and tightly fold over a small amount of the wires at each end.

EASY Steps

RINGS OF HONOR

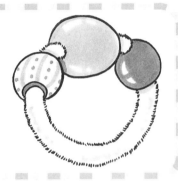

1. Give each child a piece of chenille wire, and let children slip any number of beads onto it.

2. Help each child bend the wire into a circle and tuck the ends of the wire inside one of the beads.

3. Let children adjust the rings so they will fit securely on their middle fingers.

PRESCHOOL CONNECTION

When children have finished, collect craft supplies. Open your Bible to Luke 15:11-32, and show children the passage. Tell children the parable of the prodigal son in your own words. Talk with your class about the significance of the father putting a ring on his son's finger (verse 22). Ask:

- **How did the father feel when the son came home?**
- **Why did he put a special ring on his finger?**
- **How does your Father God feel about you?**

Say: **You are so special to God. When we choose to love and follow God, he shows us his love—just like the father showed love to his son. When you wear your ring, tell your friends that you are a child of God!**

Lead children in this song, to the tune of "Ring Around the Rosy."

A ring to say, "I love you!"
I believe it is true.
God loves you, and
God loves me!

ZACCHAEUS SEES JESUS
Luke 19:1–10

What Kids Will Do: Make a tree that "grows" as they discover why Zacchaeus climbed a tree.

What Kids Will Need: newspaper, tape, scissors, green and brown paint, protective covering, baby wipes

Preparation Place: Cover a work surface with protective covering, and set out baby wipes for easy cleanup.

EASY Steps   ZACCHAEUS' TREE

1. Give each child two sheets of newspaper, and let children roll them up. Tape each roll together.

2. Help children make four cuts, about six inches long, in one end of the "tube." The slits should be evenly spaced around the end.

3. Demonstrate how to reach inside the roll and gently pull out the layers of newspaper. Preschoolers will enjoy watching the trees "grow."

4. Let children paint their trees green and brown.

PRESCHOOL CONNECTION

Have children help you clean up craft supplies. Read the story of Zacchaeus from Luke 19:1-10. Ask:

- **Why did Zacchaeus want to see Jesus?**
- **What would it be like if Jesus came to our church?**
- **What would you do to see Jesus?**

Say: **Zacchaeus knew that Jesus was special, so he climbed a tree to see Jesus! We don't have to climb trees to see Jesus; we can talk to Jesus any time we pray. Let's tell Jesus how special he is with a prayer.**

Lead children in a worship prayer. Start by praying, "Dear God, thank you for your Son, Jesus. Hear us as we tell how much we love him." Then let children take turns saying that they love Jesus. Close by saying, "In Jesus' name, amen."

Put sand in a small box, and "plant" your tree in the sand. Use toy figures to act out the story.

ZACCHAEUS SEES JESUS

Luke 19:1-10

What Kids Will Do: Make edible trees to share with others, just as Zacchaeus shared with his neighbors.

What Kids Will Need: large pretzel rods, green food coloring, frosting, small pretzel twists, paper plates, gummy bears, baby wipes, plastic wrap

Preparation Place: Mix green food coloring with frosting, then set out paper plates for the children, with a small amount of the frosting on each plate. Have children wash their hands before making this snack craft. Have baby wipes available for cleanup afterward.

EASY Steps   TREE SNACKS

1. Let children dip several pretzel twists in the frosting so they are generously covered.

2. Have each child lay a pretzel rod on his or her plate. Direct kids to stick the pretzel twists to the top of the pretzel rods so they look like the branches and leaves of a tree.

3. Allow each child to place a gummy bear "Zacchaeus" in the tree branches.

4. Cover plates with plastic wrap, and set them aside for children to take home. Allow children to make Tree Snacks they can eat during class.

PRESCHOOL CONNECTION

After children have eaten their snacks, ask them to help you clean up snack supplies. Gather children, and read Luke 19:1-10 from an easy-to-understand Bible translation. Then ask:

- **Why was Zacchaeus excited to see Jesus?**
- **Do you think Jesus was glad to see Zacchaeus? Why or why not?**
- **Do you think Jesus is glad to know you? Why or why not?**

Say: **Many people might not have liked Zacchaeus because he took money from them. But Jesus loves everyone, even though we sometimes do wrong things. Jesus wanted Zacchaeus to stop taking money from people and start doing what was right. Jesus loves us and wants us to obey God, too.**

Lead children in the following finger play:

Little Zacchaeus climbed up a tree. (*Climb your fingers up your arm.*)

Jesus was coming, and he wanted to see! (*Hold hand over eyes, as if searching.*)

Jesus looked up and said with a smile (*look up and smile*),

"Zacchaeus, I'll come to your house for a while." (*Touch fingertips together to make a roof.*)

Little Zacchaeus climbed down the tree. (*Climb your fingers down your arm.*)

His heart was now happy, as happy could be! (*Put your hands over your heart and smile.*)

ZACCHAEUS SEES JESUS
Luke 19:1–10

What Kids Will Do: Make menus for Jesus to remember that Jesus went to Zacchaeus' house to eat.

What Kids Will Need: magazine or clip art pictures of food, glue sticks, 11x17-inch sheets of construction paper, markers, scissors

Preparation Place: Cut out the magazine or clip-art pictures of food. Each child will need one full sheet and one half sheet of construction paper.

EASY Steps

A FEAST FOR JESUS

1. Give each child a full sheet and a half sheet of construction paper. Have children set the larger papers in front of them, horizontally. Let them glue the small pieces of paper vertically in the center of the larger sheets.

2. Ask children to think about what they would serve to Jesus if he came to their houses for a meal. Direct children to glue pictures of those foods to the large papers, without covering the small papers.

3. Write children's meal ideas on the smaller sheets of paper. Then fold the menus in half.

PRESCHOOL CONNECTION

Have children help you clean up craft supplies. Gather children with their menus. Read the story of Zacchaeus from Luke 19:1-10, then ask.

· **How do you think Zacchaeus felt about Jesus coming to his house?**

· **If Jesus came to your house, how would you treat him?**

· **What kinds of things can you do to show that you love Jesus?**

Say: **Zacchaeus didn't just serve Jesus a meal; he listened to Jesus! After talking with Jesus, Zacchaeus stopped taking money from people. He even gave back more money than he'd ever taken! Zacchaeus wanted to show that he loved and followed Jesus. Let's sing a song about what it means to follow Jesus.**

Lead children in the following song to the tune of "I'm a Little Teapot."

I can follow Jesus every day

When I'm at home and when I'm at play.

I will love my friends; I'll help; I'll share.

'Cause I love Jesus everywhere!

JESUS ASKS THE DISCIPLES TO REMEMBER HIM
Luke 22:7-20

What Kids Will Do: Design reminder necklaces as they learn that Jesus asked the disciples to remember him.

What Kids Will Need: plastic straws, bowl, 30-inch pieces of yarn, 3x5-inch index cards, colored markers, hole punch, scissors

Preparation Place: Cut straws into 1-inch pieces, and place them in a bowl. Then cut each index card in half. Set out supplies where children can easily reach them.

EASy Steps   REMINDER NECKLACES

1. Give each child a piece of yarn and half of an index card. Write each child's name on the back of his or her index card.

2. Ask children to draw on their cards things that remind them of Jesus. Children might draw things such as hearts, happy faces, crosses, or pictures of Jesus. Encourage children to explain their pictures.

3. Guide children in punching two holes, approximately 1 inch apart, at the center top of the card. Help children lace the yarn through the holes.

4. Children may add straw pieces to the yarn on both sides of the card, creating a "beaded" look. Tie the ends of the string, and let children wear their necklaces.

PRESCHOOL CONNECTION

Ask children to help you clean the craft area. Then open your Bible to Luke 22:7-20. Tell the story of how Jesus asked the disciples to remember him. Then ask:

- **Why did Jesus want the disciples to remember him?**
- **How do you think the disciples felt when Jesus asked them to remember him?**
- **What can *we* do to remember Jesus?**

Say: **Jesus wanted the disciples to remember him. We can remember Jesus too. Remembering Jesus helps us remember his love.**

Show children a picture of Jesus. Explain that we really don't know what Jesus looked like when he lived on earth. Pictures give us an idea of what he *might* have looked like. Ask children to close their eyes, touch their necklaces, and imagine what Jesus may have looked like to those who remembered him.

JESUS ASKS THE DISCIPLES TO REMEMBER HIM

Luke 22:7–20

What Kids Will Do: Make memory games to help them understand what it means to remember something.

What Kids Will Need: resealable sandwich bags, construction paper, ink pads and stamps, pairs of stickers, scissors

Preparation Place: Cut construction paper into 3-inch squares. Count out twelve paper squares, and place them in a sandwich bag. You'll need one sandwich bag per child.

EASY Steps — PICTURE PAIRS

1. Give each child a bag containing twelve paper squares. Then hand each child six pairs of matching stickers. Ask children to place one sticker on each square.

2. Put ink pads and stamps on the table. Direct children to decorate the backside of each square with a stamped image.

3. Ask children to place their squares in three rows, sticker side down. Show children how to turn over two squares at a time, looking for matching stickers.

4. When a match is found, allow the child to remove the pair and try again.

PRESCHOOL CONNECTION

Ask children to seal up their Picture Pairs games and set aside the bags. Then open your Bible, and review the Luke 22:7-20 story about Jesus and his disciples. Ask:

· **Why is it sometimes hard to remember things?**

· **What can you do to help yourself remember something important?**

· **What do you think the disciples might have said when Jesus asked them to remember him?**

Say: **As you played your game, you had to remember where each picture was so you could find the match. That was tricky! Sometimes we get busy playing, watching TV, or reading books and it's hard to remember Jesus. God doesn't want us to forget how much Jesus loves us or that Jesus took away our sins. Every time you play your game, you can remember to love Jesus.**

Have children form pairs and play their games. Each time a child finds a match, have him or her call out, "I remember to love Jesus."

JESUS CAME TO DIE FOR US
Luke 19:28-40; 23:1-49

What Kids Will Do: Create blocked-cheese crosses.

What Kids Will Need: 1-inch cubes of cheese, pretzel sticks, paper plates

Preparation Place: Set out supplies where children can easily reach them.

EASY Steps — CHEESE CROSS SNACKS

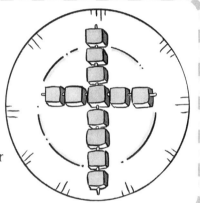

1. Give each child a paper plate.

2. Explain to the children that they will build crosses on their plates, using pretzel sticks to attach the cheese cubes. Show children how to poke the pretzel sticks into the cheese.

3. As children work, ask them to think how Jesus might have felt about dying on the cross. Then say together, "Jesus chose the cross because he loves us."

4. When children have finished building their crosses, join hands and pray. Thank God for sending Jesus to die on the cross. Then let children eat their crosses.

PRESCHOOL CONNECTION

Ask children to help you clean up. Then read portions of Luke 19:28-40 and 23:1-49, filling in the details of Christ's crucifixion. Ask:

• **What do you think Jesus thought when he heard the workmen making his cross, pounding the nails into the wood?**

• **Why did Jesus allow the people to kill him even though he hadn't done anything wrong?**

• **Why did Jesus die on the cross?**

Say: **The pretzel sticks in your snack can remind you of the sharp nails that went into Jesus' hands. Jesus hadn't done anything wrong. He didn't deserve death on a cross. But Jesus knew that it was God's plan that he would die for the world's sins. Jesus loves us and died on a cross.**

JESUS CAME TO DIE FOR US
Luke 19:28–40; 23:1–49

What Kids Will Do: Create mangers that predict the cross that Jesus would die on.

What Kids Will Need: empty matchboxes; paper plates; craft glue; brown paint; paintbrushes; 4-inch wooden craft sticks; box cutter; grass, hay, or twigs

Preparation Place: Cut the craft sticks in half with a box cutter. Pour glue onto a few paper plates to make it easier for children to use. Set out all supplies where children can reach them.

EASY Steps — MANGER PROMISE

1. Give each child a matchbox and a paper plate. Using the plates as a work surface, children may glue the box bottoms on top of the sliding box covers.

2. Direct children to paint the matchboxes brown to look like mangers. Let children talk about details of Christ's birth as they work.

3. Give each child both halves of a craft stick. Instruct children to lay the craft sticks together in the manger, gluing them in the shape of a cross.

4. Let each child glue grass, hay, or twigs in the manger at the foot of the cross. Children may also glue grass inside the matchbox covers that form the bases of the mangers.

Permission to photocopy this box from *The Encyclopedia of Bible Crafts for Preschoolers* granted for local church use.
Copyright © Group Publishing, Inc., P.O. Box 481, Loveland, CO 80539. www.grouppublishing.com

WOWS that work

Sing "Away in a Manger" with these words:

Away in a manger, no crib
for a bed;
The little Lord Jesus laid
down his sweet head.
From the beginning, God's
plan showed his love.
The Jesus who died was
God's Son from above.

PRESCHOOL CONNECTION

Let children clean up while their crafts dry. Open your Bible to Luke 19:28-40 and 23:1-49. Show children the words, then paraphrase the story given in those Scriptures. Ask:

· **Why was Jesus born?**

· **What kind of life did Jesus live as he grew up?**

· **How would you feel about being punished because of the bad things *someone else* had done?**

Say: **God knew that the world would need a Savior—someone to save us from all the bad things we do. So God sent Jesus to be born and laid to sleep in a manger. As Jesus grew up, he didn't do anything wrong. He never sinned. Jesus died on the cross to take away *our* sins so we could live forever with God.**

JOHN

JESUS TURNS WATER INTO WINE

John 2:1–11

What Kids Will Do: Make colorful jars to remind themselves of how Jesus turned water into wine.

What Kids Will Need: white glue, paintbrushes, water, shallow bowls, grape powdered drink mix, empty salt shakers, empty and clean baby food jars, newspaper, permanent marker

Preparation Place: Cover the craft table with newspaper. Pour glue into several shallow bowls, and dilute it with enough water to make the glue runny. Pour the powdered drink mix into salt shakers. Set the bowls, paintbrushes, and baby food jars on the table.

EASY Steps — WONDERFUL WINE VATS

1. Give each child a baby food jar, and write his or her name on the bottom, using permanent marker.

2. Show children how to brush the diluted glue over the outside of the jar. (Children should paint one section at a time rather than cover the entire jar at once.)

3. Have the children carefully shake the powdered drink mix over the wet glue.

4. When children have covered the jars with purple drink mix, set the jars aside to dry.

PRESCHOOL CONNECTION

When children have finished, have them help you clean up the craft supplies. Then gather children on the floor. Read aloud John 2:1-11 from an easy-to-understand Bible translation. Then ask:

· **How do you think the people felt when they ran out of wine?**

· **Why do you think Jesus helped the people?**

· **What are some special ways that Jesus helps you?**

Say: **These jars remind us how Jesus made people happy by turning plain old water into a special, yummy drink. Nobody can do that but Jesus! Jesus can do anything because Jesus is God's Son.**

WOWS that work
When the jars are completely dry, you may want to take them outside and spray them with a coat of clear acrylic.

JESUS TURNS WATER INTO WINE

John 2:1–11

What Kids Will Do: Make super snacks to remind them that God can make great things out of our disappointments.

What Kids Will Need: resealable plastic bags, chocolate cookies such as Oreos, bowls of chocolate pudding (you can substitute vanilla yogurt for a healthier alternative), plastic spoons

Preparation Place: At a table, set out a plastic spoon and a bag for each child. Set out bowls of pudding where children can easily reach them.

EASY Steps — FROM GARBAGE TO GREAT

1. Give each child three cookies. Have the children place the cookies in their bags and seal the bags.

2. Guide children in talking about things that make them sad. Point out that sometimes when we're sad, we say that we're "brokenhearted." Let children pound the bags with their fists to crush the cookies, to show the way sadness makes our hearts feel broken.

3. Talk about how Jesus can change our sad times into happy times. Have children spoon pudding into their bags. Help reseal the bags, and let children mix the pudding and the cookies together.

4. Have children open their bags and enjoy their yummy snacks.

PRESCHOOL CONNECTION

When children have finished, have them help you clean up the craft supplies. Then gather children on the floor. Read aloud John 2:1-11 from an easy-to-understand Bible translation. Then ask:

· **Why do you think Jesus helped the sad people?**

· **Who helps you when you feel sad?**

· **How does it feel to know that Jesus can help us when we are sad?**

Say: **The people who were throwing the wedding party were sad. They ran out of wine to share with all of their friends. But Jesus changed plain old water into wine. Jesus can change things that make us sad, too.**

JESUS TURNS WATER INTO WINE

John 2:1–11

What Kids Will Do: Make butterflies to remind themselves that Jesus can make everything new.

What Kids Will Need: large, white tube socks; colorful felt; wiggly eyes, scissors, Glue Dots (Glue Dots are available at most craft and hobby stores.)

Preparation Place: For each child, cut two 8-inch butterfly wing shapes from the felt.

EASY Steps

A CHANGE FOR THE BETTER

1. Give each child a tube sock, and help children turn it inside out. Show children how to use the Glue Dots to attach wiggly eyes near the toes of the socks. (Press the Glue Dots to the socks, then let children add the eyes.)

2. Let children turn the socks right side out. Instruct them to use Glue Dots to attach two more wiggly eyes near the toes of the socks.

3. Distribute butterfly wings. Direct children to use Glue Dots to attach the wings on either side of the sock. (You may find it easier for children if you wear the sock puppet while they attach the wings.)

4. Show children how to turn the sock inside out to show the fuzzy "caterpillar" side. Then let them turn the caterpillars inside out and watch them change into butterflies.

Permission to photocopy this box from *The Encyclopedia of Bible Crafts for Preschoolers* granted for local church use.
Copyright © Group Publishing, Inc., P.O. Box 481, Loveland, CO 80539. www.grouppublishing.com

PRESCHOOL CONNECTION

When children have finished, have them help you clean up the craft supplies. Then gather children on the floor with their butterfly puppets. Read aloud John 2:1-11 from an easy-to-understand Bible translation. Then ask:

· **In this story, how did Jesus change an "ugly" time into a happy time?**

· **How do you think the people felt when Jesus changed water into wine?**

· **How can Jesus help you when you have a sad or "ugly" time?**

Say: **Just like the caterpillar changes from a plain, little bug into a beautiful butterfly, Jesus can change our sad times into wonderful, glad times! Let's wave our butterflies and thank God for helping us when we're sad.**

Let children wear their butterfly puppets as you lead a simple prayer of thanks.

You may want to provide scraps of felt that children can attach to the butterfly wings. Encourage children to make the wings as bright and colorful as possible.

JESUS CLEARS THE TEMPLE TO WORSHIP GOD

John 2:13-22

What Kids Will Do: Make celebration sticks to use as they praise God at church.

What Kids Will Need: paint stir sticks, crepe paper strips, tape, markers, shoe laces, large jingle bells, scissors, CD player, children's worship music CD

Preparation Place: Cut the crepe paper into 12-inch strips. Set all supplies where children can easily reach them.

EASY Steps — CELEBRATION STICKS

1. Let children use the markers to decorate the paint sticks.

2. Direct children to choose three or four crepe paper strips, and have children tape the strips to the paint stir sticks.

3. Help each child string one or two jingle bells on the shoelace, pulling the bells to the center of the shoelace.

4. Pull the ends of the shoelaces even, then have children help you tape the ends to their paint sticks. The jingle bells should hang down, away from the sticks, on the shoelaces.

PRESCHOOL CONNECTION

When children have finished, collect craft supplies. Open your Bible to John 2:13-22, and show children the passage. Tell children the story in your own words. Talk with your children about why Jesus wanted the merchants to leave the temple. Ask:

· **Who did Jesus want to leave the temple?**

· **What kinds of things did Jesus want people to do in the temple?**

· **What kinds of things do we do in our church?**

Say: **God wants us to celebrate and worship in his house, not use it as a place to make money! Let's wave our celebration sticks as we worship and praise God.**

Play a children's worship CD, and lead children in waving their colorful music celebration sticks.

JESUS CLEARS THE TEMPLE TO WORSHIP GOD

John 2:13-22

What Kids Will Do: Make yummy, edible bags of coins.

What Kids Will Need: baby wipes, hot dogs, pita bread, ketchup, mustard, mayonnaise, knife

Preparation Place: Cut the hot dogs into thin slices. Mix the ketchup, mustard, and mayonnaise in a ratio of 2:1:1. Cut a strip off the top of each piece of pita bread to make a "bag."

EASY Steps — BAGS OF COINS

1. Let children clean their hands with baby wipes.

2. Give each child a pita "bag," and help kids carefully pull the sides open.

3. Direct children to add a few hot dog slices as coins to the bags.

4. Children may "spend" their coins by taking them out of the bag, dipping them in the condiment mixture, and eating them.

PRESCHOOL CONNECTION

When children have finished, collect craft supplies. Open your Bible to John 2:13-22, and show children the passage. Tell children the story in your own words. Ask:

· **What were the merchants in the temple doing with their money?**

· **What did Jesus want people to be doing in the temple?**

· **How does your church use the money you bring to the church?**

Say: **When we bring our money to the church, our church can use it to help people. We want to show others God's love. But the men in our Bible story weren't using the money to help anyone but themselves! It's good to give our money back to God.**

WOWS that work

Lead children in the following song to the tune of "The Muffin Man."

Can I share a coin with you,
A coin with you,
A coin with you?
Can I share a coin with you
To show you our God's love?

JESUS CLEARS THE TEMPLE TO WORSHIP GOD
John 2:13–22

What Kids Will Do: Build temples to remember that God's house is a special place.

What Kids Will Need: empty individual juice or milk cartons, craft sticks, glue, construction paper, markers, scissors

Preparation Place: Thoroughly wash and dry the milk or juice cartons. Cut the construction paper into rectangles that will just cover the sides and top of the cartons.

 **MY OWN TEMPLE**

1. Give each child a juice carton. Help children glue construction paper onto the tops and sides of the cartons.

2. Children may use markers to draw doors and windows on the "temples."

3. Demonstrate how to glue the craft sticks on the front of the temple as pillars.

4. Have children draw people standing near the doors of the temples.

PRESCHOOL CONNECTION

When children have finished, collect craft supplies. Open your Bible to John 2:13-22, and show children the passage. Tell children the story in your own words. Ask:

· **What did Jesus want people to do in the temple?**

· **What do we do in our church?**

· **What things are special about our church?**

Say: **These temples you made are special reminders of God's house. Jesus knew that God's house was special too. He wanted everyone to treat the temple in a special way. You can use your craft to remember to always treat our church as God's special house.**

Instead of glue, construction paper, and craft sticks, use frosting, graham crackers, and pretzel sticks. Yum!

JESUS EXPLAINS ETERNAL LIFE TO NICODEMUS

John 3:1-21

What Kids Will Do: Make Peekaboo Nicodemus figures.

What Kids Will Need: sealed small envelopes, sealed business-size envelopes, gray and yellow crayons, marker, scissors

Preparation Place: Set out supplies on a table where children can easily reach them.

EASY Steps   PEEKABOO NICODEMUS

1. Give each child two sealed small envelopes. Let them cut a small strip off one end of each of the envelopes. Children may cut the business-size envelope so it is about the same length as the smaller envelopes. This will leave one end of each envelope open.

2. Let children use markers to draw pictures of sad Nicodemus on the business-size envelopes. Then have children color the faces gray to show that he came to Jesus in the dark.

3. Let each child use a marker to draw a happy Nicodemus on one small envelope. Kids may draw a happy Jesus on their other small envelopes. Children should color these faces with yellow crayons to show that Jesus came to bring light—or to show the way to God.

PRESCHOOL CONNECTION

When children have finished, collect craft supplies. Open your Bible to John 3:1-21, and show children the words so they know the passage is in God's Word. Have children slip their happy Nicodemus puppets inside the sad Nicodemus puppets.

Say: **Nicodemus came to Jesus in the dark. There were lots of things about God that he didn't understand.** Have each child put the "double" Nicodemus puppet on one hand and the Jesus puppet on the other hand. Let children show how Nicodemus went to visit Jesus. **Jesus told Nicodemus many important things about God's love. Jesus didn't want Nicodemus to be sad.** Let children remove the darker puppet to reveal the yellow puppet. **Jesus wanted Nicodemus to see the light and learn more about how much God loves us!** Ask:

· **Why did Nicodemus go to Jesus?**

· **Do you have questions about God? What are they?**

· **How can you find out answers to your questions?**

Say: **We can find many of our answers in God's Word, the Bible! We can also ask teachers and parents to help us understand God. Jesus came to help us all see how much God loves us. Let's pray and thank God for sending Jesus.**

Lead children in prayer, thanking God for the gift of Jesus.

Lead children in this simple finger play to help children understand why Jesus came to earth.

One, two, Jesus loves you! (Hold up one finger, then two fingers.)

Two, three, he died for you and me. (Add another finger.)

Three, four, don't be sad anymore! (Add another finger.)

Four, five, now Jesus is alive! (Wiggle all five fingers.)

183

JESUS EXPLAINS ETERNAL LIFE TO NICODEMUS
John 3:1-21

What Kids Will Do: Make mobiles depicting John 3:16.

What Kids Will Need: craft foam, fabric scraps, cotton balls, glue, yarn, masking tape, stickers of Jesus, scissors, pens

Preparation Place: Cut one of each of the following shapes out of fun foam for each child: a red heart, a blue circle, an oval, a brown cross, a white cloud. Cut the yarn to 6-foot lengths.

EASY Steps — JOHN 3:16 MOBILES

1. Read John 3:16 to the children from your Bible. Then give each child a set of shapes.

2. On the red hearts, let older preschoolers write, "God" in pen. (You can have the words written ahead of time for younger preschoolers.) Let children draw green land on the blue circles to represent "For God so loved the world." Then add their names. Direct each child to take one length of yarn and tape the shape to one end of the yarn.

3. Let each child draw a happy face on the oval and glue on a fabric scrap for clothing, to represent "that he gave his one and only Son." Encourage each child to place a sticker of Jesus on the cross to represent "that whoever believes in him." Direct each child to take two more lengths of yarn and tape each shape to one end of a piece of yarn.

4. Children can glue cotton balls to the clouds to represent "shall not perish but have eternal life." Let children tape these shapes to one end of the remaining lengths of yarn. Make a loop at the other end. Fold all of the yarn lengths in half, and knot them at the midsection. Use the loop to hang the mobile.

PRESCHOOL CONNECTION

After they have completed the craft, teach the children this paraphrase of John 3:16: "God loved everyone in the world so much that he gave us his Son, Jesus. If you believe in Jesus, you will live in heaven forever." Have the children point to the symbols as they repeat the verse after you. Ask:

- **Why is this such an important verse to remember?**

- **How do you feel knowing that God loves you so much that he gave you Jesus?**

- **What can you do to show that you love God?**

Say: **God loves us so much that he gave his only Son, Jesus, to us. God let Jesus be born as a baby, grow up, and be hung on a cross to die. God wants to forgive us for all the bad things we do. God wants us to be in heaven with him forever!**

WOWS that work

Use an instant-print camera to take a picture of each child. Let children glue their pictures to the "world" pieces of the mobiles.

JESUS EXPLAINS ETERNAL LIFE TO NICODEMUS

John 3:1–21

What Kids Will Do: Make Bible bookmarks.

What Kids Will Need: poster board, clear tape, crayons, 6-inch lengths of ribbon, hole punch, mini magnifying glasses (found in the party section of many craft stores), scissors

Preparation Place: Cut poster board into 2x6-inch strips. On each strip of poster board, write, "I Spy More About God!"

EASY Steps "I SPY" BOOKMARKS

1. Give each child a poster board strip. Read the words aloud, and explain that kids will be making something to help them learn more about God.

2. Set out crayons, and let children color their poster board strips with things they know about God.

3. Help each child use the hole punch to make a hole at the top of the strip.

4. Let each child slip a length of ribbon through the hole, and help him or her tie a knot. Then tie a magnifying glass to the other end of the ribbon.

PRESCHOOL CONNECTION

When children have finished, collect craft supplies. Read John 3:1-21 aloud from an easy-to-understand Bible translation so children know the passage is in God's Word. Then ask:

- **Why did Nicodemus come to Jesus?**
- **What do you do when you have questions about God?**
- **Who helps you know more about God and Jesus?**

Say: **We all have questions about God and Jesus. That's why God gave us the Bible, his own Word! When someone reads the Bible to you, you can use your bookmark to show them things you want to know about. Just use your magnifying glass to point out pictures of things that you have questions about. It's good to learn all we can about God!**

JESUS TALKS WITH A SAMARITAN WOMAN

John 4:4-26

What Kids Will Do: Create the Samaritan woman at the well.

What Kids Will Need: 9x12-inch sheets of card stock, scissors, glue stick, craft foam, paper cups, chenille wires, tape, hole punch, pens or pencils

Preparation Place: For each child, cut two triangles with a 4-inch base and one circle the size of the paper cup bottom. Make several foam templates of these shapes.

EASY Steps — BROKEN AND HEALED WOMAN

1. Demonstrate how to hold the card stock horizontally and fold two sides backward. Crease the paper well and then open it. Children will form the woman in the middle section.

2. Direct children to glue the tips of the triangles together on the card stock to form the woman's body. They can glue the circle "heads" to the top triangles. Allow children to draw smiles and hair on the women's heads.

3. Punch a small hole near each of the woman's shoulders. Let each child slip a chenille wire through the holes to make arms. Punch two holes in each cup. Children may twist the arms to hold the cups. Demonstrate how the "water jug" can move up to her mouth and down.

PRESCHOOL CONNECTION

When children have finished, collect craft supplies. Open your Bible to John 4:4-26, and show children the passage. Tell children the story in your own words. Then ask:

- **Why was the woman so sad?**
- **How did Jesus help the woman feel happy again?**
- **When has Jesus helped you feel happy?**

Say: **The woman who met Jesus at the well had her life in many pieces—she was sad. When she believed in Jesus, she became whole and happy. We can come to Jesus with all of our questions, all of the bad things we do, and all of our thoughts. Jesus will forgive us and make us whole, like the pieces of a puzzle.**

WOWS that work

Let the children fill the women's water jugs with real water, using an eyedropper. Talk about how Jesus meets our needs.

JESUS TALKS WITH A SAMARITAN WOMAN

John 4:4-26

What Kids Will Do: Make thirst-quenching gifts to give.

What Kids Will Need: new, unopened water bottles; large paper labels; markers; stickers; gift tags; curling ribbon; scissors; hole punch

Preparation Place: Cut the curling ribbon into 12-inch lengths. Punch a hole in one side of each gift tag. Set all other supplies where children can reach them.

EASY Steps   WATERY GIFTS

1. Give each child a bottle, and instruct him or her not to open it. Let children put the large labels on their bottles.

2. Direct children to decorate the labels with markers and stickers.

3. Help each child write the name of someone special on the gift tag. Then slip the curling ribbon through the hole, and help each child tie it around the neck of the bottle. Curl the ribbon.

PRESCHOOL CONNECTION

When children have finished, collect craft supplies. Open your Bible to John 4:4-26. Tell children the story in your own preschool-friendly words. Then ask:

· **What do you think the woman came to get at the well?**

· **What did the woman learn about Jesus?**

· **What wonderful things do you know about Jesus?**

Say: **The woman at the well didn't know who Jesus was. She didn't know that Jesus was God's special Son. She didn't know that Jesus already knew all of her sad feelings. Jesus helped the woman feel better—not because he gave her plain old water. Jesus healed the woman's sad heart. Jesus can help us feel new again too. When you give this water to a friend, tell him or her some of the wonderful things you know about Jesus.**

Give children a salty snack, such as pretzels or saltine crackers. Talk about it feels to be thirsty. Ask children what it would be like to have to go without water. Then give each child a drink of cool water. Talk about how good it feels to drink the water. Point out that Jesus makes our hearts feel like that when we give our sadness to him.

JESUS TALKS WITH A SAMARITAN WOMAN
John 4:4-26

What Kids Will Do: Make cards to invite others to come to church.

What Kids Will Need: construction paper, colorful stickers, envelopes, markers, stamps, glue, scissors, photocopies of church information

Preparation Place: Have each child bring the name and address of one friend he or she would like to invite to church. Type out and photocopy information about your church, such as programs for families, service times, and other special information.

EASY Steps
"SOME WILL COME" INVITATIONS

1. Give each child a colorful sheet of construction paper. Have children glue the church information to the bottom half of their papers.

2. Allow children to fold the paper in half so the church information is inside. Then let children decorate their invitations with stickers, markers, and other colorful additions.

3. Have the children put their invitations into envelopes. Address the envelopes to children's friends. (If children didn't bring addresses, simply let children hand-deliver the invitations.)

PRESCHOOL CONNECTION

When children have finished, collect craft supplies. Open your Bible to John 4:4-26, and show children the passage. Tell children the story in your own words. Then ask:

- **After the woman met Jesus, what did she ask the people to do?**
- **Why was the woman so happy?**
- **How can you invite more people to learn about Jesus?**

Say: **After the Samaritan woman met Jesus, she ran to the people in her town and said, "Come, see a man who told me everything I ever did. Could he really be the God we've been wanting?" Some came to Jesus. Some came and believed that Jesus is God's Son.**

There are many people who don't know Jesus. They are just waiting for someone to invite them to church. If we do our part and tell people who Jesus is, God will do his work in their hearts.

WOWS that work

Have a "Come to Jesus" party. Bring in balloons, treats, and streamers. Play upbeat worship music, and help children celebrate the joy of bringing friends to church. Talk about how important it is to tell others about Jesus, just like the Samaritan woman did.

JESUS FEEDS FIVE THOUSAND
John 6:1–15

What Kids Will Do: Make baskets to remind them of Jesus' miracle.

What Kids Will Need: 8½x5½-inch sheets of brown construction paper, 1-inch strips of tan construction paper, stapler, glue sticks, scissors

Preparation Place: Set the brown papers in front of you horizontally. Then make three slits across each paper, leaving a ½-inch frame around the edges.

EASY Steps

WOVEN BASKETS

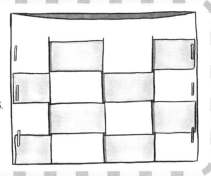

1. Give each child a piece of brown paper and seven tan strips.
2. Demonstrate how to weave the tan papers through the slits in the brown paper.
3. Help children use glue sticks to glue the ends of the tan strips to the brown papers.
4. Fold the woven paper in half, then staple two sides to form a pocket or "basket."

PRESCHOOL CONNECTION

After the children have cleaned up, read aloud John 6:1-15 from an easy-to-understand Bible translation. Then ask:

· **How did Jesus feed so many people with just a few loaves of bread and some fish?**

· **Why do you think Jesus fed all the people?**

· **How does Jesus show you his love today?**

Say: **Jesus did a miracle to show how mighty he was. Jesus made so much food that they had to put the leftovers in baskets. He also fed the people to show that he loved and cared for them. Jesus loves and cares for us today, too! When you use your basket at home, you can remember all the ways Jesus shows his love to you.**

For extra fun, give the children fish-shaped crackers to fill up their baskets.

JESUS FEEDS FIVE THOUSAND
John 6:1–15

What Kids Will Do: Make fun fish to remember how Jesus cared for the hungry people.

What Kids Will Need: acetate or clear plastic page protectors, brightly colored tissue paper, staplers, scissors

Preparation Place: Cut a fish shape, approximately 7x4 inches, from two pieces of acetate. Cut tissue paper into small strips, ½x12 inches. You'll need one pair of fish for each child.

EASY Steps

FANCY FISH

1. Give each child two fish, and have children stack their fish together. Let children help you staple all around the edges of the fish, leaving a 2-inch opening along one edge.

2. Have children stuff the fish shapes with the tissue-paper strips, using a variety of colors.

3. When children are satisfied with their fish, staple the openings shut.

PRESCHOOL CONNECTION

When children have finished, collect craft supplies. Read John 6:1-15 aloud from an easy-to-understand Bible translation so children know the passage is in God's Word. Then ask:

· **How do you think the people felt before Jesus fed them?**

· **How do you think they felt after they saw Jesus feed so many people with just a little food?**

· **Tell about a time Jesus took care of you.**

Say: **Jesus saw all those hungry people and wanted to help them. He did an amazing thing by feeding so many people with just a few fish and loaves of bread. Jesus takes care of you every day. He gives you people to love and care for you. He provides food and a warm bed. Jesus loves you so much!**

Let children take their fish home to remind them to ask Jesus to help them with all their needs.

JESUS FEEDS FIVE THOUSAND
John 6:1–15

What Kids Will Do: Make loaves of bread as they learn how Jesus fed many people with just a little food.

What Kids Will Need: frozen roll dough, baking sheet, spray cooking oil, brown paper grocery sacks, baby wipes, marker, scissors, oven

Preparation Place: Before class, allow the dough to thaw according to package directions. Cut the paper sacks into 3x5-inch pieces, and write each child's name on a piece of brown paper.

EASY Steps — YUMMY BREAD

1. Give each child a baby wipe, and ask children to clean their hands. Then give each child a piece of roll dough.

2. Have children shape the dough into oblong loaf shapes.

3. Let each child set his or her loaf on a greased baking sheet. Place the brown paper with the child's name slightly under his or her loaf.

3. Bake according to package directions. Be sure to allow loaves to cool before kids enjoy them.

PRESCHOOL CONNECTION

While the little loaves are cooking, read the story of Jesus feeding five thousand from John 6:1-15. Talk with children about how much food the little boy had in his lunch and how that much would never have fed so many people. Remind them that the little boy gave all he had to Jesus. Ask:

- **Why do you think the boy gave Jesus his lunch?**
- **What did Jesus do with the boy's lunch?**
- **What can you give to Jesus?**

When the loaves have cooled, let the children pray to thank Jesus. Let children enjoy their yummy bread!

To make this activity even more mouth-watering, have butter and honey available to spread on the warm bread.

JESUS WASHES THE DISCIPLES' FEET
John 13:1-17

What Kids Will Do: Design serving trays as they learn how Jesus showed his disciples how to serve others.

What Kids Will Need: aluminum biscuit pans, white paint, paintbrush, tempera paint, paper plates, rubber craft stamps, embroidery thread, craft glue, marker, snacks

Preparation Place: A few days before this activity, paint each aluminum pan white. On the day of the craft, squeeze a little paint onto several paper plates, and place these within children's reach.

EASY Steps   SERVING TRAYS

1. Give each child a white aluminum pan. Write each child's name on the bottom of his or her pan.

2. Guide children in lightly dipping rubber stamps in paint and then pressing the stamp once or twice on a paper plate to remove excess paint.

3. Let children stamp designs on the white pans.

4. To trim pan edges, children may glue embroidery thread around the perimeter. As children work, let them brainstorm ideas for using their trays.

PRESCHOOL CONNECTION

While trays dry, ask children to assist you in cleaning up and putting away craft supplies. Open your Bible to John 13:1-17, and tell the story of Jesus washing his disciples' feet. Then ask:

- **What does it mean to serve someone?**
- **Why do you think Jesus washed the disciples' feet?**
- **What do you think Jesus hoped the disciples would learn about serving?**

Say: **Jesus washed the disciples' feet to show them how much he loved them. He wanted his disciples to learn to serve and love others too. Jesus wants us to serve and love people, just like his disciples did. We can show love by serving and helping others.**

Let the children serve each other snacks, using the trays they just made.

JESUS WASHES THE DISCIPLES' FEET

John 13:1–17

What Kids Will Do: Make aprons to remind them to serve others.

What Kids Will Need: 9x12-inch pieces of white felt, hole punch, yarn, tempera paints, paper plates, sponge shapes, scissors

Preparation Place: Pour a thin layer of paint onto several paper plates. Use the hole punch to make holes (about 2 inches apart) across the longer side of each piece of felt. Set out all other supplies where children can easily reach them.

EASY Steps — ACTION APRONS

1. Give each child a piece of white felt and a 4-foot length of yarn.

2. Direct children to lace yarn through the holes, creating apron "strings."

3. Allow children to dip the sponges in the paint and stamp patterns on their aprons.

PRESCHOOL CONNECTION

When children have finished, ask them to help you collect the craft supplies. Discuss the John 13:1-17 account of Jesus washing the disciples' feet. Ask:

· **Can you name some things you can do to put this apron "into action"?**

· **When you serve others, how do you think it makes them feel?**

· **How does serving someone else make *you* feel?**

Say: **We can grow in love by serving others. Jesus was a servant; he came to take away our sins and show us God's love. Jesus set an example for us to follow. We can be like Jesus and serve others with love.**

that work

Let children don their aprons and launch into cleaning their meeting room. Toys should be put away, floor can be swept, and furniture may be dusted. Small toy brooms actually do "work," and socks worn over hands make fun dusters.

ACTS

GOD SENDS HIS HOLY SPIRIT

Acts 2:1–21; 3:12–19

What Kids Will Do: Make edible flames to represent the tongues of fire that appeared at Pentecost.

What Kids Will Need: ice cream cones, vanilla ice cream, ice cream scoops, red and yellow sprinkles, chocolate chips or raisins

Preparation Place: Set up the craft items like an assembly line. Place the ingredients in the following order: cones, ice cream and scoops, chocolate chips or raisins, red and yellow sugar sprinkles.

EASY Steps — FLAVORFUL FLAMES

1. Help each child scoop one scoop of ice cream into a cone.
2. Next, let children add chocolate chips or raisins to make a person's eyes and mouth.
3. Have children shake the red and yellow sprinkles on top of the ice cream to represent the tongues of fire.

PRESCHOOL CONNECTION

Open your Bible to Acts 2:1–21; 3:12–19, and tell the story of Pentecost in your own words. As children use their tongues to lick the ice cream cones, talk about the tongues of fire that came down. Explain that people heard and understood Peter in their own languages. Then ask:

• **Can any of you say words in another language?**

• **How do you think the people felt when they could understand Peter in their own language?**

• **Who can you tell about Jesus, using your words?**

Say: **Peter's words were very special. He was telling everyone about Jesus. Let's say a prayer for the people that we want to tell about Jesus.**

Lead the children in prayer, allowing each child to mention the name of the person he or she wants to tell about Jesus.

GOD SENDS HIS HOLY SPIRIT
Acts 2:1-21; 3:12-19

What Kids Will Do: Make pinwheels to remind them of the wind that blew at Pentecost.

What Kids Will Need: Pinwheel Pattern (p. 196); card stock; red, yellow and orange crayons; hole punch; drinking straws; scissors; tape

Preparation Place: Photocopy a pinwheel pattern from page 196 onto card stock for each child. Set out a pinwheel for each child, and place other supplies in the center of the table to be shared.

EASY Steps   WIND POWER

1. Let children cut out the square pinwheel pattern and use the crayons to color both sides of the pinwheel to look like flames.

2. Show children how to cut along the dotted lines. Use a hole punch to make holes in the center and four corners where marked. (An adult will need to do this step.)

3. Have children each thread the pinwheel onto the straw, starting with the center and then bringing up the corners from A to D. Place tape over the last point to hold it closed.

4. Direct children to push the pinwheel to the center of the straw, holding onto the ends. Blow into the cupped points, rather than straight on.

PRESCHOOL CONNECTION

Have the children hold their pinwheels in their laps. Read Acts 2:1-21; 3:12-19 from a preschool-friendly Bible translation. Review the section of the story when the mighty rushing of wind comes. As you talk about the wind, encourage the children to blow on their pinwheels to make them spin. Ask:

· **What does it sound like on a windy day?**

· **How do you think the people felt when they heard the mighty wind?**

· **Who can you think of the next time you hear the wind?**

Lead the children in prayer, thanking God for the wind and what it represented on the day of Pentecost.

PINWHEEL PATTERN

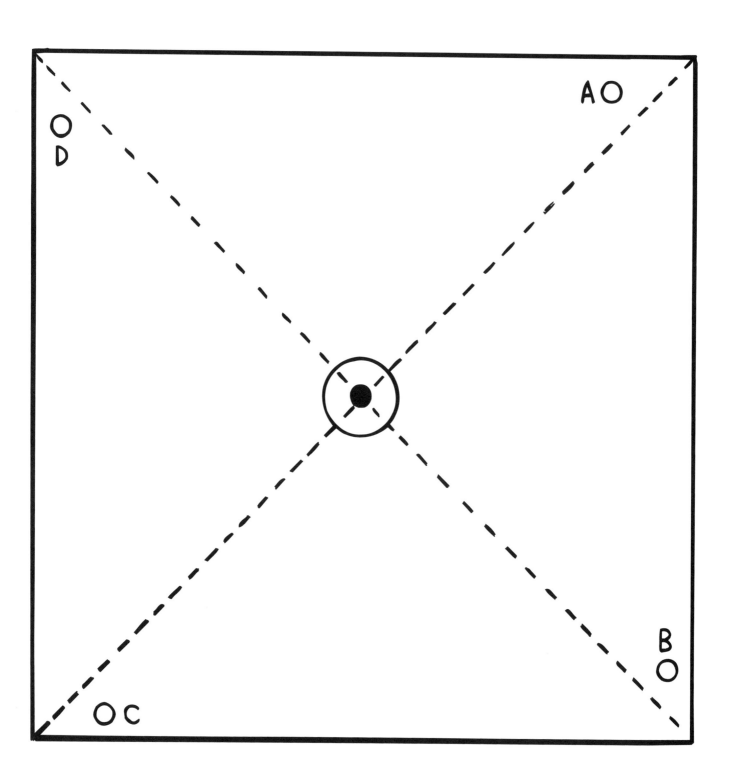

GOD SENDS HIS HOLY SPIRIT
Acts 2:1-21; 3:12-19

What Kids Will Do: Make puppets that remind them of the story of Pentecost.

What Kids Will Need: large craft sticks, coffee filters, watercolor markers, spray bottles, yarn, child-safe scissors, tape, paper towels, permanent marker

Preparation Place: Use a permanent marker to draw a simple face on one end of each craft stick. On a table, place a double layer of paper towels at a spot for each child. Lay two coffee filters, one craft stick, and an 8-inch piece of yarn at each place. Fill several spray bottles with water, and have several pairs of child-safe scissors. Have extra paper towels on hand.

EASY Steps   HOLY SPIRIT FILLED PETER

1. Have each child color the first coffee filter with yellow, red, and orange markers to make fire. Each child may color the second filter with any color he or she chooses.

2. Let children lay one filter on the paper towels and gently spray it with water. Set the filter aside, and have children spray their other filters. Use an extra paper towel to blot the filters dry.

3. Help children fold the filters in half and then in half again, making a pie shape. Show children how to cut the orange filter at an angle across the large end and cut the tip off the second filter.

4. Direct children to open the orange filter, gather the middle, twist the end, and tape it to the top of the craft stick above the face. Slide the other filter onto the lower portion of the stick, forming a "robe," and tie it on with yarn.

PRESCHOOL CONNECTION

Put all craft supplies away, and gather children around you. Read Acts 2:1-21; 3:12-19 from an easy-to-understand Bible translation. Allow children to hold up their puppets when they hear about the tongues of fire. Then ask:

- **Why is it dangerous to play with fire?**
- **Why did the people in the story not get burned by the fire?**
- **How do you think the people felt being a part of such a special day?**

Say: **God sent fire as a way of showing that his helper, the Holy Spirit, was there with the people that day. God helped Peter do a hard job, telling lots of people about Jesus that day. God will help us do hard things too. Let's hold up our puppets and thank God for his power and help.**

Lead children in cheering, "Thank you, God!"

Allow the children to be really creative with their puppets by supplying other items such as yarn for hair or chenille wires for arms.

THE ANGEL FREES PETER FROM JAIL
Acts 12:1–18

What Kids Will Do: Make bread chains that they can break as they learn how an angel saved Peter from jail.

What Kids Will Need: refrigerator bread sticks, cookie sheets, oven, wax paper, plastic knives

Preparation Place: Lay out a piece of wax paper for each child to work on, and place a plastic knife at each place.

EASY Steps

BREADSTICK CHAINS

1. Give each child two breadsticks, and have him or her cut each one in half to form four pieces.

2. Show children how to roll one piece of dough into a "snake" and then pinch the ends tightly together to form a circle.

3. Let children continue rolling each piece of dough and looping it through the previous circle to form a chain. Be sure children pinch each end tightly so the chain stays together.

4. Help children transfer their chains to a cookie sheet. Bake the chains according to package directions, watching carefully so they don't burn.

PRESCHOOL CONNECTION

While the bread chains bake, have children wash their hands and then gather children around you. Open your Bible to Acts 12:1-18, and let children act out the story as you read it. Then ask:

· **How would you feel if your hands were in chains?**

· **How do you think Peter felt when his chains fell off?**

· **What do you think the guards thought when they woke up and Peter was gone?**

Say: **God sent an angel to free Peter from jail. God took good care of Peter, and God wants to take care of us. God sends loving parents, helpful teachers, and Christian friends who help us—just as the angel helped Peter. When you eat your bread chains, you can break them apart and remember that God sends help to us, too.**

WOWS that work

Before baking the chains, allow children to brush them with melted butter and then sprinkle them with cinnamon sugar or Parmesan cheese. Or serve the baked chains with melted cheese for dipping.

THE ANGEL FREES PETER FROM JAIL

Acts 12:1–18

What Kids Will Do: Make chains to go on their wrists, just like Peter might have worn.

What Kids Will Need: colorful paper clips, plastic milk jugs, hole punch, colored pencils, scissors, permanent marker

Preparation Place: Cut circles from a plastic milk jug, using the lid as a size guide. Make a hole in the top of each disk. Use a permanent marker to draw a very simple angel on each circle. You'll need one disk for each child.

EASY Steps COLORFUL CHAINS

1. Give each child approximately sixteen colored paper clips. Demonstrate how to loop the clips together by placing the large outer loop over the smaller inside loop.

2. Once children have hooked several clips together, check for size, then help each child hook one end to the other to form a bracelet.

3. Let children wear their chain bracelets as they color the angel disks with colored pencils.

4. Let each child slide a paper clip through the hole in the angel disk and then hook it onto the bracelet for a charm.

PRESCHOOL CONNECTION

Let children wear their chains while you read Acts 12:1-18 aloud from an easy-to-understand Bible translation. Then ask:

· **What would be the worst thing about having to wear chains around your wrists?**

· **What do you think Peter's chains would have been like?**

· **How do you think he felt when the chains fell off?**

Say: **Most likely, Peter wasn't very comfortable when he wore chains. But the chains you made today are light and pretty! They also have angels on them to remind you that God sent an angel to help Peter. God helps us every day. Let's pray and thank God for loving us and helping us.**

Have the children hold hands to form a sort of chain, then lead them in prayer.

If you don't have enough milk jugs to make the charms, lightweight cardboard, poster board, or card stock would also work. Older children may also draw their own angels.

THE ANGEL FREES PETER FROM JAIL
Acts 12:1–18

What Kids Will Do: Make zip-line toys to remind them that the angel freed Peter from jail.

What Kids Will Need: white card stock, yarn, crayons, drinking straws, tape, paper clips, scissors

Preparation Place: Cut two 36-inch pieces of yarn, one 3x8-inch strip of card stock, and one 2½-inch straw for each child. Set all supplies in center of table for children to share.

EASY Steps   ZIP-LINE PETER

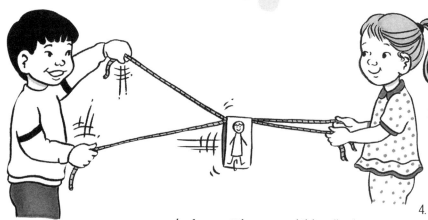

1. Give each child a piece of card stock, and instruct children to fold it in half. Then have children color an angel on one side and Peter on the other.

2. Help children tape the straw into the fold and use the paper clip at the bottom of the card stock to hold both sides together.

3. Guide children as they slide both pieces of yarn through the straw.

4. Form pairs and have each child hold one end of yarn. When one child pulls the two yarn pieces apart, it will send the angel to the other end. Then the partner can pull his or her yarn apart and send it back.

that work

To make it easier for the children to slide the yarn pieces through the straws, tape the two pieces of yarn together at one end. This will make the end stiff enough that it will slide right through. Cut off the tape once the children have the yarn through the straws.

PRESCHOOL CONNECTION

When children have finished, collect craft supplies. Read Acts 12:1-18 from a preschool-friendly Bible translation. Then ask:

- **Who leads you places when you go out?**
- **Who was leading Peter out of jail?**
- **Why do you think Rhoda was so surprised to see Peter at her house?**

Say: **Let's play with our craft one more time and pretend that one person is the jail and the other person is Rhoda's house. When I say "pull," we will move the angel and Peter down the street. Ready? Pull!** Allow the children to take several turns sending the paper back and forth.

LYDIA IS CONVERTED
Acts 16:9-16

What Kids Will Do: Make purple crosses as they learn how Lydia learned about God.

What Kids Will Need: several shades of purple construction paper, 6x9-inch sheets of card stock, markers, child-safe scissors, glue sticks, hole punch, yarn

Preparation Place: Use a marker to draw a cross pattern on a sheet of card stock for each child. To make the pattern, make a thick cross on one side of the card stock. This is the side to which children will glue paper. Turn over the card stock, and draw a thinner cross shape right behind the first one. Set out all the supplies on a table.

EASY Steps   LYDIA'S CROSS

1. Have the children tear the construction paper into small pieces. Be sure that every child has a variety of different shades.

2. Let children glue the pieces onto the thicker cross pattern, overlapping the pieces and making sure they cover the entire area.

3. Help children turn the card stock over and cut out the cross on the lines.

4. Punch a hole in the top of the cross, and tie a piece of yarn through to make a hanger.

PRESCHOOL CONNECTION

When children have finished, collect their crafts and set them to the side. Read Acts 16:9-16 from an easy-to-understand Bible translation. Then ask:

- **What is your favorite color? What do you think was Lydia's favorite color?**
- **Who did Lydia believe in?**
- **How did Lydia show everyone that she believed in Jesus?**

Say: **Today we made purple crosses to remind us that Lydia believed in Jesus, that he died and rose again. We can believe in Jesus too! Let's pray and thank God for his Son, Jesus.**

Lead children in prayer, thanking God for sending Jesus to die on a cross.

LYDIA IS CONVERTED
Acts 16:9–16

What Kids Will Do: Weave purple place mats to remember that Lydia sold purple cloth.

What Kids Will Need: 8½x11-inch sheets of felt in 2 different shades of purple, scissors (If you want to have children glue the ends of the felt strips, you'll need Glue Dots. Glue Dots are available at most craft and hobby stores.)

Preparation Place: Cut slits lengthwise into one color of felt, approximately 1 inch apart, leaving a 1-inch uncut border all the way around the edge. Cut the other color of felt lengthwise into 1-inch strips. Set the pieces on a table.

EASY Steps

WEAVERS

1. Demonstrate how to weave the felt strips over and under.

2. Give each child one sheet of felt with slits and approximately seven pieces of felt with which to weave.

3. Help children weave their place mats, then trim the weaving pieces to the size of the mat.

4. Children may wish to glue the ends of each strip to the felt (using Glue Dots) or leave unglued so they can weave it again and again.

PRESCHOOL CONNECTION

Open your Bible to Acts 16:9-16, and tell children the story in your own words. Then ask:

- **What do you think is the hardest thing about being a weaver?**
- **Why do you think Lydia chose to weave and sell purple fabric?**
- **Who can you invite to use your purple place mat and tell about Lydia?**

Say: **Lydia sold purple cloth to help her family have money. But she helped her family even more when she told them about God's love. The Bible tells us that Lydia's whole family was baptized when they heard Paul teach about Jesus! Whenever you use your purple place mat, you can remember to tell your family members about Jesus too.**

If you have someone in your church who has a weaving loom, invite him or her in to show how it works. Maybe they could even weave something purple!

LYDIA IS CONVERTED

Acts 16:9–16

What Kids Will Do: Dye vanilla pudding different colors.

What Kids Will Need: instant vanilla pudding, milk, containers with lids, spoons, bowls, food coloring, measuring cups

Preparation Place: Set up a table for every four children. Each station will need a box of pudding, a measuring cup, milk, and a container with a lid. Set the bowls, spoons, and food coloring aside.

EASY Steps PUDDING DYE

1. Help each group pour its pudding mix into the container, add the correct amount of milk, and take turns shaking the pudding for approximately five minutes until thick.

2. While the pudding sets for an additional five minutes, give each child a spoon and two bowls.

3. Scoop one-fourth of the pudding into each child's first bowl, and let children add several drops of coloring. Make sure that each child at the table has a different color pudding.

4. Once the pudding has been dyed, use the second bowl to share scoops of different-colored pudding between each child at the table.

PRESCHOOL CONNECTION

As the children enjoy their dyed pudding snacks, read Acts 16:9-16 from an easy-to-understand Bible translation. Then ask:

· **What happened when we added the food coloring to the pudding?**

· **Do you think Lydia dyed the fabric that she sold in the same way or in a different way?**

· **The pudding changed when we added the coloring. How do people change when they believe in and love God?**

Say: **We don't know a lot about Lydia, but we do know that she sold purple fabric and that she loved God. God's love changed Lydia's life forever! She believed in God, and she and her whole family were baptized. God's love can change us, too.**

PAUL AND SILAS GO TO JAIL
Acts 16:16–34

What Kids Will Do: Make first-aid kits as they learn how the jailer took care of Paul and Silas.

What Kids Will Need: clean, empty plastic icing containers; plastic adhesive bandages; cotton swabs; pre-moistened packaged wipes; gauze pads; card stock; crayons; tape; scissors; marker

Preparation Place: Cut the card stock into strips that will wrap around the icing containers (approximately 3½x10 inches). Use a marker to write, "First-Aid Box" in the center of the card stock, leaving a space above to add each child's name. The children will need to work at a table for this project.

EASY Steps — FIRST-AID BOXES

1. Give each child a container and a strip of card stock. Write each child's name on his or her strip, and then allow children to decorate the strips with crayons.

2. Help each child tape one end of the strip to the container and then wrap the paper around the container and tape down the other end securely.

3. Let each child add two adhesive bandages, two cotton swabs, one gauze pad, and one pre-moistened wipe to his or her container.

WOWS that work

Set out stuffed animals and dolls, cloth bandages, baby wipes, and adhesive bandages. Let children lovingly clean and bandage the animals and dolls. Encourage children to tell the toys, "I want to show you God's love."

PRESCHOOL CONNECTION

Clean up craft supplies, and have children set their First-Aid Boxes aside. Read aloud Acts 16:16-34 from an easy-to-understand Bible translation. Then ask:

• **Have you ever helped someone who was injured? What did you do to help?**

• **Why do you think the jailer helped Paul and Silas?**

• **How do you think Paul and Silas felt when the jailer helped them?**

Say: **The jailer wasn't a friend of Paul and Silas, but he showed love by cleaning and bandaging their cuts. We can show God's love when we help those who are hurt. You can use your First-Aid Boxes to show people how much God loves us.**

PAUL AND SILAS GO TO JAIL

Acts 16:16–34

What Kids Will Do: Make edible jails to remember that Paul and Silas were put in prison.

What Kids Will Need: small pretzel sticks (not rods), cheese cubes, paper plates, E.L. Fudge cookies

Preparation Place: Set out all of the items on a table where children can easily reach them.

EASY Steps PRETZEL JAILS

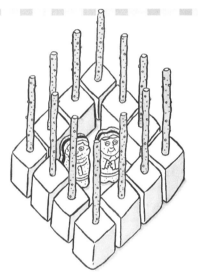

1. Give each child a paper plate. Let each child count out twelve cheese cubes, twelve pretzel sticks, and two cookies.

2. Direct children to stick one pretzel into each cheese cube and then set the pretzels in a square to form a jail.

3. Children may place Paul and Silas (the E.L. Fudge cookies) in the jail.

4. Let children gently shake their plates to make an earthquake, causing the bars to fall down.

PRESCHOOL CONNECTION

As the children enjoy their snack, tell the story from Acts 16:16-34 in your own words. Then ask:

· **What do you think it would feel like to be in an earthquake?**

· **What do you think Paul and Silas were thinking during the earthquake?**

· **What did the jailer think had happened to all the prisoners?**

Say: **Even though an earthquake can be scary, God was still with Paul and Silas. God even sent a kind jailer who cared for Paul and Silas. God is with us all the time, even when we're scared. We can trust that God will take care of us every day.**

Show children how to hug themselves tightly as they pray, "Thank you, God, for loving me and caring for me every day. In Jesus' name, amen."

PAUL AND SILAS GO TO JAIL
Acts 16:16–34

What Kids Will Do: Make soap carvings that remind them of the songs Paul and Silas sang.

What Kids Will Need: bars of Ivory Soap, metal spoons, wax paper, small resealable bags, knife, marker, songbook

Preparation Place: Before class, use a knife to draw a simple musical note on each bar of soap. (The pattern should take up the entire bar.) On a table, set out a large piece of wax paper, a bar of soap, a spoon, and a bag for each child.

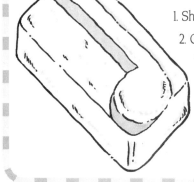

EASY Steps — MUSICAL-NOTE SOAP

1. Show the children the songbook, and talk about the musical notes.

2. Guide children in using the handles of the spoons to trace around the pattern on the bars of soap.

3. Help children scrape out around the pattern so the musical note is raised up higher than the rest of the soap. Children may use their fingers to smooth out the soap.

4. Have children place their bars of soap in plastic bags, making sure that each child's name is on his or her bag.

PRESCHOOL CONNECTION

Clean up craft supplies, and have children set their crafts aside. Read aloud Acts 16:16-34 from an easy-to-understand Bible translation. Then ask:

· **Do you ever sing songs while taking a bath? What is your favorite song to sing?**

· **What kind of songs do you think Paul and Silas liked singing?**

· **What do you think the jailer thought about Paul and Silas' songs? Why?**

Say: **Even though Paul and Silas were in jail, they still wanted to praise God with songs. Maybe those songs helped them remember God's loving care, or maybe the songs reminded them that God would be with them. Paul and Silas worshipped God, even during a hard time. We can remember to praise and worship God all the time!**

Lead the children in singing several songs of praise. Then remind them that when they use their soap to take a bath this week, they can sing songs and remember Paul, Silas, and the kind jailer who washed them.

Make sure that you have extra bars of soap on hand in case a bar breaks. Younger children may require a bit of extra help tracing the shape onto the soap and defining the shape.

PAUL IS SHIPWRECKED
Acts 27:1-44

What Kids Will Do: Make biscuit boats as reminders of the boat Paul sailed on.

What Kids Will Need: refrigerator biscuits, baking sheets, oven, large paper plates, pretzel sticks, block cheddar cheese, teddy bear–shaped cookies, square cheese crackers, knife

Preparation Place: Cut each biscuit in half, and bake according to package directions. On the table, set out two paper plates for each child, cheese triangles, pretzel sticks, teddy bear–shaped cookies, and square cheese crackers.

EASY Steps — PAUL'S BOAT

1. Give each child two biscuit halves and two paper plates.

2. Let each child set one biscuit half on each plate. Point out that the semicircle looks like a little boat.

3. Help each child stick a pretzel stick into the flat "top" of each boat to create a mast. Then show children how to lay a cheese triangle on a pretzel stick to form a sail.

4. Children may set bear cookies in each boat, then place square cheese crackers around to represent cargo boxes thrown overboard.

PRESCHOOL CONNECTION

Let children hold one of their boats while you tell the story of Paul's shipwreck from Acts 27:1-44. (They'll take the other boat home to help tell family members what they've learned.) As you get to the part about the shipwreck, have the children take a bite of their boats. When you have finished the story, allow the children to finish eating their boats while you ask them the following questions.

· **Can you tell me about a time you have ridden in a boat?**

· **How did the men who were in the boat with Paul feel?**

· **How did Paul know that everything was going to be OK?**

Say: **Paul knew that the only way everyone would be saved was if they followed God's directions. You and I can follow God's directions too. We can obey the words in the Bible. We can listen and learn about God from our parents and teachers. We can pray and ask God to help us obey during hard times. Let's say a fun prayer right now.**

Have children link arms and sway from side to side, as if they're on a rocking boat. Lead children in prayer, asking God to help them obey.

PAUL IS SHIPWRECKED

Acts 27:1-44

What Kids Will Do: Create magnetic dioramas depicting Paul's shipwreck.

What Kids Will Need: shoe boxes; sandpaper; blue, brown, white, and gray construction paper; glue sticks; paper clips; scissors; heavy duty magnets; crayons; tape

Preparation Place: Set a shoe box top or bottom at each child's place. Place other materials where they will be easily accessible to all the children.

EASY Steps — STORY IN A BOX

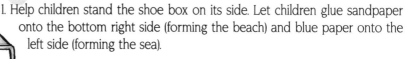

1. Help children stand the shoe box on its side. Let children glue sandpaper onto the bottom right side (forming the beach) and blue paper onto the left side (forming the sea).

2. Direct children to color the inside back of the box, making waves above the sea and rocks above the sand. Children may cut the gray paper into cloud shapes and glue them into the box.

3. Help each child cut a boat from the brown paper and draw Paul on the white paper. Have kids cut him out and glue him into the ship.

4. Let each child tape three paper clips to the back of the boat. Show how to hold a magnet to the back of the box and move it around so that the boat will "sail" in the sea and then crash into the rocks and sand.

PRESCHOOL CONNECTION

Open your Bible to Acts 27:1-44, and tell children the story in your own words. As you tell the story, allow the children to act it out with their shoe box crafts. Then ask:

· **Can you tell me about a time you were very afraid?**

· **How did the men on the boat with Paul behave when they were afraid?**

· **Who was protecting Paul and the other sailors?**

Say: **Paul went through lots of scary times—on the ocean, in prison, and even shipwrecked! But Paul never forgot that God was with him. I'm glad that God is with us, too. We can always trust that God is with us.**

PAUL IS SHIPWRECKED
Acts 27:1-44

What Kids Will Do: Make colored sand pictures of the Bible story.

What Kids Will Need: photocopies of the "Paul's Shipwreck" handout (p. 210), 8x10-inch sheets of cardboard (or heavy duty poster board), glue sticks, various colors of sand, small shells and rocks, fish-shaped craft foam, plastic spoons, newspaper, small bowls

Preparation Place: Make a photocopy of the "Paul's Shipwreck" handout from page 210 for each child. Cover a table with newspaper, and place small bowls of colored sand, rocks, shells, and foam cutouts around.

EASY Steps   SHIPWRECK SAND ART

1. Give each child a "Paul's Shipwreck" handout and a sheet of cardboard. Let children use glue sticks to glue the picture to one side of the cardboard.

2. Have children rub a relatively thick layer of glue on one section of the picture and then sprinkle sand onto that section. Help children shake excess sand back into the bowl.

3. Direct children to repeat step two until the entire picture is covered with (and colored with) sand.

4. Children may glue small shells and rocks onto the beach and fish-shaped craft foam onto the sea. Allow children to draw Paul in the boat.

PRESCHOOL CONNECTION

Open your Bible to Acts 27:1-44, and tell children the story in your own words. Then ask:

· **Can you tell me about time you played in the sand or at the beach?**

· **How do you think the men felt when they were safely on the beach?**

· **Why do you think God kept Paul and the others safe?**

Say: **I imagine that when the men felt that soft sand under their feet, they were pretty thankful to be ashore! Your sand pictures can remind you to thank God for all the ways he keeps us safe. Let's go around the circle and tell some ways God keeps us safe.**

When each child has had a turn, close by saying, "Thank you, God, for keeping us safe."

that work

Instead of doing the craft project and then telling the story, have the children make their projects as you tell the story, gluing whatever section you are talking about at that time.

PAUL'S SHIPWRECK

FAITHWEAVER™ BIBLE CURRICULUM INDEX

SCRIPTURE INDEX

HANDS-ON™ BIBLE CURRICULUM INDEX

For more amazing resources

visit us at
www.group.com...

...or call us at
1-800-747-6060 ext. 1370!

Group
Incredible things will happen™